CABINET
WAR ROOMS

BY PETER SIMKINS

Imperial War Museum 1983
Copyright © The Trustees of the
Imperial War Museum
Reprinted 1984

ISBN 0-901627-28-3

Filmset and printed by
BAS Printers Limited,
Over Wallop, Hampshire

Designed by
Grundy and Northedge Designers

COVER ILLUSTRATIONS
FRONT: The Map Room
IWM 82/20/20 C
BACK: The Cabinet Room
IWM 82/20/67 C

CONTENTS

The Cabinet War Rooms are the surviving and most important portion of the underground emergency accommodation provided for Mr Churchill's Cabinet and its chief military advisers during the Second World War. It is fortunate indeed that this historic site has remained more or less exactly as it was at the end of the war and the Imperial War Museum is very pleased to be associated with the Government's project to restore the Rooms and to open them to the public as a museum.

The Imperial War Museum, which is the national museum responsible for recording the history of twentieth century conflicts involving British and Commonwealth forces, has contributed historical advice and conservation expertise to the restoration work and has undertaken to manage the Cabinet War Rooms on a day-to-day basis as the agent of the Property Services Agency of the Department of the Environment.

To preserve the historical integrity and unique atmosphere of the War Rooms it has been decided to keep the number of explanatory labels to a minimum. Essential information about each room is provided in a guide-leaflet issued to every visitor at the beginning of his tour. The purpose of this booklet, which has been written by the Museum's Historian, Mr Peter Simkins, is to provide our visitors with a more detailed account of the history, origins and role of the Cabinet War Rooms and to explain the development in Britain of Cabinet machinery for the higher direction of war during the first half of the twentieth century. The booklet is based on extensive research into unpublished documentary, photographic and personal evidence.

Visitors to the Cabinet War Rooms and readers of this booklet may like to be reminded that they can pursue their study of the Second World War and other conflicts since 1914 in the exhibitions, reference collections and archives of the Imperial War Museum at its headquarters in Lambeth Road, London SE1 and its outstations, HMS *Belfast* in the Pool of London and Duxford Airfield in Cambridgeshire.

Alan Borg
Director
Imperial War Museum
October 1983

2

ABOVE View of the western side of the Government Offices, Great George Street, formerly known as the New Public Offices. The Cabinet War Rooms are situated in the basement below this side of the building, which faces St James's Park. From December 1940, Winston Churchill occupied a suite of rooms, called the 'No. 10 Downing Street Annexe', on the ground floor of the building. The windows of these rooms can be seen to the right of the main entrance on the St James's Park side as one looks at this photograph. *IWM 82/20/177*

INTRODUCTION

The Cabinet War Rooms, which served as the principal emerg-ency accommodation for the British War Cabinet and Chiefs of Staff in the Second World War, are situated in the western base-ment of the Government Offices, Great George Street, formerly known as the New Public Offices. These rooms offer a unique in-sight into the manner in which the British Government organised itself for war in the first half of the twentieth century and of the machinery which it established for the higher direction of the nation's war effort in the struggle against Germany, Italy and Japan between 1939 and 1945. To understand the full significance of the Cabinet War Rooms and the important place which they occupy in the history of the Second World War, it is therefore necessary to look first at the origins, development and functions of the various bodies which they were intended to protect.

THE CABINET AND ITS ROLE IN GOVERNMENT ▬▬

In Britain today, the power to make laws, or legislate, is vested in Parliament, which consists of the Queen, the House of Lords and the House of Commons. The real legislative authority rests with the House of Commons, the part of Parliament which is elected at regular intervals by the people. However, the country is actually governed by the Prime Minister and the other ministers of the Crown. Following a general election, the leader of the dominant party in the Commons is summoned by the Sovereign to form a Government as Prime Minister. The Prime Minister, in turn, nominates the ministerial heads of the various Government departments. The supreme directing body of the Government is the Cabinet, which is essentially an inner circle of ministers whom the Prime Minister chooses to consult frequently on matters of general policy. Its membership is not fixed but it invariably includes the principal officers of State such as the Foreign Secretary and the Chancellor of the Exchequer. The Cabinet determines the overall national policy for home and foreign affairs, draws up the legislative programme for its current term of office and co-ordinates the work of the different Government departments. Executive power is held, not by a Government department, but by its minister, who is individually accountable to Parliament for his actions. Ministers also share a collective responsibility for the Government's policy and, to ensure the unity of the executive, are expected to support all Cabinet decisions.

THE CABINET AND DEFENCE IN THE NINETEENTH ▬▬ CENTURY ▬▬

It was not until the Reform Act of 1832 and the transfer of political sovereignty to the electorate that the Cabinet truly began to assume its present form. In the sphere of national and imperial defence, the Cabinet, apart from taking the decision to wage war when the need arose, now incurred the ultimate responsibility for the size and equipment of the armed forces and the deployment of troops and fleets. In fact, once Napoleon had been defeated, the first half of the nineteenth century was a comparatively peaceful period for Britain. No great power seriously threatened the British Isles or the Empire won in the colonial wars of the previous century and, with the supremacy of the Royal Navy unchallenged, seaborne commerce flourished, contributing to Britain's economic ascendancy over other nations. As a result, military questions aroused only sporadic interest in the party politics of the day and successive Cabinets kept military and naval expenditure to a minimum, paying little heed to the efficiency of the services. Between 1854 and 1858 the Crimean War and the Indian Mutiny exposed grave weaknesses in Britain's military organisation and provided some impetus for improvements in military administration over the next fifteen years. Edward Cardwell, the Secretary of State for War in W E Gladstone's Cabinet of 1868 to 1874, introduced a major series of reforms, including the reorganisation of the War Office, which paved the way for a more professional British Army. On the other hand, the main guardian of national and imperial security – the Royal Navy – was allowed to deteriorate for want of money and attention until the late 1880s.

The underlying problem was that, because neither service yet possessed a proper strategic planning staff, there was no organ short of the Cabinet which could examine all aspects of defence and recommend a coherent policy for all departments. Without such advice, most Cabinet ministers were ill-equipped to deal effectively with defence questions. In the last quarter of the century recurrent tension with Russia along the North-West Frontier of India, French and Russian naval building programmes and the growing power of a unified Germany highlighted the need for a balanced British defence policy. At the same time Britain was obliged to embark upon a fresh phase of imperial expansion in response to a scramble by European nations for colonies in Africa and elsewhere. As the burdens of governing a complex industrial society and protecting the Empire multiplied, increasing use was made of the committee system, which not only eased the pressure of business on the Cabinet itself but also offered ministers a means of obtaining the continuous and detailed advice from experts that was necessary for successful long-term planning.

Fears of a war with Russia in 1878 led the Conservative Government of Benjamin Disraeli to set up the Colonial Defence Committee, a body of officials from the Admiralty, the War Office, the Colonial Office and the Treasury, whose task was to consider how best to safeguard vital colonial ports. Revived in 1885 as a standing committee, it advised the colonies on the broad principles of imperial strategy and kept their respective local defence schemes under constant review, suggesting appropriate modifications in the light of notable changes on the international scene or in the technology of warfare. The Colonial Defence Committee thus supplied some continuity of planning from one administration to another and, through the work of G S Clarke, its Secretary until 1892, evolved procedures which were adopted by later bodies of this type. However, being composed of relatively junior officials, its influence remained limited as long as the spirit of co-operation between Government departments, especially between the Admiralty and War Office, was missing.

By the mid-1890s, colonial rivalries and the growth of European alliances were beginning to accentuate Britain's international isolation. In 1895 a Conservative Government took office under Lord Salisbury, whose nephew Arthur Balfour, an advocate of inter-service co-ordination, became First Lord of the Treasury and Leader of the House of Commons. Salisbury was therefore prompted to establish a standing Defence Committee of the Cabinet with the Lord President of the Council, the Duke of Devonshire, as chairman. Besides Balfour, the new body included the First Lord of the Admiralty, the Secretary of State for War and the Chancellor of the Exchequer. It was empowered to consider defence questions in general and appeared to carry enough political weight to make the service departments and other ministries work more closely together, yet it failed to fulfil its promise. It met irregularly; it had no permanent secretariat, so there were no accurate records of its proceedings; the omission of key figures such as the Prime Minister and Foreign Secretary meant that contentious issues still had to be referred to the full Cabinet; the professional heads of the services attended only to give information on certain points, not to take part in discussions; and in the continued absence of adequate planning staffs, its members were confined to dealing with financial matters and specific inter-departmental disputes instead of shaping future policy.

THE COMMITTEE OF IMPERIAL DEFENCE ■■■■■■■

The shortcomings of Britain's defence organisation were revealed once more in the South African War of 1899–1902 but the country's inability to bring about the speedy surrender of the Boers was not the sole reason for anxiety at the turn of the century. In particular, Germany, the strongest land power in Europe, was now constructing a battle fleet designed to mount a direct challenge to the Royal Navy in the North Sea. Against this background, Britain started to rebuild and modernise her armed forces and overhaul the machinery for the higher direction of military and naval policy. The Committee of Imperial Defence (CID) was established in December 1902 when Balfour, who had succeeded Salisbury as Prime Minister that summer, recast the Defence Committee of the Cabinet to include senior officers from the services as well as Cabinet ministers. At first Balfour attended its meetings as an ordinary member, the Duke of Devonshire acting as chairman until the autumn of 1903.

While this body represented a positive advance, a committee headed by the influential Lord Esher was appointed in November 1903 to make recommendations for the reconstitution of the War

ABOVE Arthur Balfour (1848–1930).
As Prime Minister from 1902 to 1905,
Balfour was one of the principal archi-
tects of the Committee of Imperial
Defence. During the First World War he
served as First Lord of the Admiralty from
May 1915 to December 1916 and then
became Foreign Secretary in Lloyd
George's administration. He was created
an Earl in 1922. *IWM Q41928*

Office and, in January 1904, expressed doubts about the existing structure of the CID, which it saw as 'the cornerstone of the needed Edifice of Reform'. Accordingly, in May 1904, the CID was remodelled on the lines suggested by Esher and his colleagues. The Prime Minister became the chairman and, initially, the only permanent member of the CID, although Esher too was made a permanent member in 1905. The Prime Minister had absolute discretion in the choice of other members, so giving the Committee much greater authority and flexibility. Simultaneously, the ability of the CID to tackle problems continuously and in depth was vastly strengthened by the creation of a full-time secretariat. From this point until the outbreak of the Second World War, with a break only during the First World War when its work was absorbed by other bodies, the Committee served as the principal advisory body on every aspect of home and overseas defence.

The CID had no executive or administrative functions, and its proposals were submitted either to the Cabinet or the departments concerned for further action. It formulated the general principles on which defence policy should be based and prepared plans to ensure that naval, military and civil authorities at home and abroad would respond in a co-ordinated manner if war were declared, tasks made easier by the creation of a General Staff for the Army in 1906 and of a Naval Staff in 1912. After 1906, much of the work of the CID was delegated to sub-committees, which could take the detailed evidence of expert witnesses and investigate more fully questions of a technical or controversial nature. Four of the sub-committees were permanent, the most important of these being the Committee on the Co-ordination of Departmental Action, which produced the War Book, a comprehensive list of the measures to be taken both by the Cabinet and by individual departments in the event of hostilities.

Up to August 1914 the full Committee of Imperial Defence met, with varying frequency, in Disraeli's old home at 2, Whitehall Gardens. The Prime Minister and Esher were usually present, as were the service ministers, their senior professional advisers, the Chancellor of the Exchequer and the Secretaries of State for Foreign Affairs, India and the Colonies. Other ministers attended if the problems being discussed were relevant to their departments and elder statesmen, members of the Opposition and outside specialists were invited if it was felt that they could make a useful contribution. Inevitably, when defence questions came before the Cabinet, several of its leading members already held views moulded by the advice of experts at meetings of the CID. Hence the deliberations of the Committee of Imperial Defence were of fundamental importance in the framing of defence policy.

As Esher had foreseen, the permanent secretariat proved to be an

ABOVE Sir Maurice (later Lord) Hankey at his desk at No. 2 Whitehall Gardens. He is wearing the Full Dress uniform of a Colonel in the Royal Marine Artillery for this formal photograph. Born in 1877, Hankey served in the Royal Marine Artillery before being appointed Naval Assistant Secretary of the Committee of Imperial Defence in 1908. He was Secretary of the Committee of Imperial Defence from 1912 to 1938, Secretary to Lloyd George's War Cabinet from 1916 to 1919 and Secretary to the Cabinet from 1919 to 1938. Although he endeavoured to maintain a degree of neutrality appropriate to these posts, his position at the centre of political and military affairs caused him to become a confidential adviser, particularly on strategic matters, to successive Prime Ministers. He was appointed Minister without Portfolio in Chamberlain's War Cabinet in September 1939 and held this office until the following May. He died in 1963. *Courtesy of the Cabinet Office*

indispensable part of its structure. When a matter was referred to the CID or one of its sub-committees, the secretariat prepared, or obtained from other departments, any necessary memoranda bearing upon the subject under review. On receipt of the Prime Minister's instructions to call a meeting, the secretariat then drew up an agenda and circulated it to those summoned, together with the relevant papers. Minutes of every meeting, containing a concise summary of the discussion and the conclusions reached, were produced and sent to members within twenty-four hours. After the minutes were approved, extracts were sent to the departments concerned for appropriate action. Copies of all memoranda were kept in five main series and each series was bound, titled and dated in such a way that the secretariat could quickly find any document that might be required. Thus by 1914 the CID secretariat had developed a system for the orderly conduct of business in a field which involved more than one Government department.

The first Secretary of the Committee of Imperial Defence was Sir George Clarke, formerly the Secretary of the Colonial Defence Committee. At the outset there were also two Assistant Secretaries, nominated by the Admiralty and War Office respectively, and a small clerical staff. Three more Assistant Secretaries had been added by 1912. Clarke was succeeded by Sir Charles Ottley in 1907, and in 1912 Captain Maurice Hankey, the Naval Assistant Secretary since 1908, took over the post, Hankey, the moving spirit behind the compilation of the War Book, was destined, like Clarke, to leave an indelible mark on British constitutional practice.

CABINET GOVERNMENT IN THE FIRST WORLD WAR ■■■

With the coming of war in August 1914, the Committee of Imperial Defence fell into abeyance. The smoothness of Britain's mobilisation demonstrated the value of the War Book but it was soon realised that the CID had not been equally far-sighted in other directions. Mainly because of the prevailing belief that the war against Germany would be short there was no similar blueprint for the expansion of the Army or the provision of adequate reinforcements, despite Britain's commitment to a continental land campaign, and insufficient study had been devoted to the conversion of industry to war purposes. The CID had also failed to anticipate that Cabinet control of the war could not be exercised effectively without further reorganisation of the machinery of government.

In 1914 the Cabinet under H H Asquith, the Liberal Prime Minister since 1908, numbered twenty and was, in effect, too big to meet every day or to assemble at short notice. A smaller body, able to react more swiftly to the pressures of modern war, was clearly needed and in November 1914 Asquith set up a special Cabinet committee, known as the War Council, to explore particular aspects of war policy and to review the overall strategic situation. Apart from Asquith, it included Field-Marshal Lord Kitchener, the Secretary of State for War, and Winston Churchill, the First Lord of the Admiralty, as well as Sir Edward Grey, the Foreign Secretary, and David Lloyd George, the Chancellor of the Exchequer. Balfour, now a member of the Opposition, was brought in because of his long experience on the CID, and the Chief of the Imperial General Staff and the First Sea Lord were regular attenders. Within four months its membership had grown to thirteen and the previous disadvantages of having too large a directing body recurred. Furthermore, Asquith insisted on maintaining the collective responsibility of the Cabinet and ordained that, if the War Council proposed any basic changes in policy, the approval of the full Cabinet must be secured, even though several ministers had little direct interest in operations.

Following the formation of a coalition government in May 1915, the War Council gave way to the Dardanelles Committee, comprising four Liberal and five Conservative ministers. The Dardanelles Committee, originally intended to deal with operations in that theatre, was gradually drawn into considering wider strategic issues and, like its predecessor, increased in size. In November 1915 it was replaced by a five-man War Committee, but the membership of the latter rose to nine before the end of the year and even higher during 1916. The War Committee was more involved than its two forerunners in the daily conduct of naval and military operations and in this respect it assumed greater executive power. In all three cases, however, the tendency to grow bigger defeated the primary object of such committees, while the retention of ultimate authority by the full Cabinet, and the consequent necessity for additional discussion, delayed the implementation of decisions. Hankey and the staff of the Committee of Imperial Defence acted as a secretariat to the War Council and its successors but the Cabinet itself had no secretariat at this date, the only record of its proceedings being contained in a private letter sent by the Prime Minister to the Sovereign after each meeting. As Hankey later recalled, ministers 'sometimes misapprehended the decisions, and the staffs of the Admiralty and War Office and the Civil Service chiefs were often in the dark as to what had been decided and what action they had to take'.

As the mounting demands of the war led the War Committee deeper into the complicated problems of manpower, shipping, food supply and industrial output, the drawbacks of divided responsibility and the lack of a Cabinet secretariat were even more keenly felt. When Lloyd George replaced Asquith as Prime Minister in December 1916, he immediately combined the functions of the War Com-

ABOVE David Lloyd George (1863–1945). Having served as Chancellor of the Exchequer from 1908 to 1915, Lloyd George was appointed Minister of Munitions in the coalition government formed in May 1915. In July 1916 he moved to the War Office as Secretary of State for War and succeeded Asquith as Prime Minister in December that year. The small War Cabinet which he set up on becoming Prime Minister provided a model for the War Cabinets of Neville Chamberlain and Winston Churchill during the Second World War. He was granted an Earldom in the New Year's Honours list for 1945 and died in March 1945, less than two months before the end of the war in Europe. *IWM Q70208*

mittee and the Cabinet by creating a small War Cabinet. This was composed of Lloyd George himself, Andrew Bonar Law as Chancellor of the Exchequer, Lord Curzon, Lord Milner and Arthur Henderson, then leader of the Parliamentary Labour Party. The South African soldier and statesman, General J C Smuts, joined the War Cabinet in 1917. Since Bonar Law alone had departmental responsibilities, the remainder were able to give their whole attention to the tasks of direction and co-ordination. Similarly, ministers no longer in the Cabinet had more time to devote to their exacting departmental duties. They still attended those War Cabinet discussions which concerned their departments but they now had no share in collective Cabinet responsibility for the conduct of the war. In theory, therefore, authority was concentrated into the hands of a single small body although in reality it was redivided in other ways. Some questions were delegated to individual War Cabinet ministers, who were given *ad hoc* committees of officials and departmental ministers to help them. Standing committees, with War Cabinet ministers presiding, were set up to co-ordinate the policies of departments whose spheres of interest frequently intersected. Finally, in recognition of the need to separate war planning from daily administration, inner committees of the War Cabinet were created to determine strategy, an outstanding example being the War Policy Committee, comprising Lloyd George, Curzon, Milner and Smuts, which was established in June 1917 to review plans for the coming offensive in Flanders. The result was that, whether acting as a single body or by delegating tasks to individual members, Lloyd George's War Cabinet tended to operate as a kind of supreme court, arbitrating between the various Government departments and its own inner committees.

The establishment of the War Cabinet in December 1916 was accompanied by the formation of a Cabinet secretariat under Hankey, who had been knighted earlier that year. Hankey turned the secretariat of the Committee of Imperial Defence into an organisation which served the Cabinet as a whole and which, in due course, became the Cabinet Office. For the first time, Cabinet meetings were attended by a Secretary who kept a record of proceedings and communicated decisions to the appropriate departments. This was perhaps the most long-lasting of all the innovations in governmental machinery which stemmed from the First World War.

THE CHIEFS OF STAFF COMMITTEE

The War Cabinet was superseded by a peacetime Cabinet of normal size in November 1919 and the Committee of Imperial Defence was revived in its original form. Hankey stayed on as Secretary to both the Cabinet and the CID. Before it was dissolved the War Cabinet instructed the service departments to assume that the British Empire would not be engaged in any other great war during the next ten years. This assumption was endorsed by the Cabinet and CID periodically and, until it was rejected in 1932, the possibility of a major conflict was officially deemed, on any given day, to be at least ten years distant. Though the 'ten-year rule' acted as a powerful curb on defence preparations, it remained the duty of the CID to advise the Cabinet as to how Britain's defence organisation should be adapted to take account of the lessons of 1914–1918 and to meet the changed conditions of the post-war world. Prior to the First World War there had been only two fighting services, but the creation of the Royal Air Force as an independent service in 1918 made the business of co-ordination not only more vital but also infinitely more complex.

To achieve proper inter-service co-operation, the Chiefs of Staff Sub-Committee of the Committee of Imperial Defence was formed in 1923. Henceforth, in addition to tendering separate advice on questions of sea, land and air policy, the First Sea Lord, the Chief of the Imperial General Staff and the Chief of the Air Staff had an individual and collective responsibility for advising on defence policy as a whole. The Prime Minister was nominally chairman of this body but, in the main, the Chiefs of Staff met alone with one of their number, designated by the Prime Minister, in the chair. In spite of intermittent friction over certain aspects of defence policy, such as the control of naval aviation, the Chiefs of Staff Committee facilitated close and continuous consultation between the services and was soon the most important element in the CID. In Hankey's own words: 'The Secretariat was still "the cornerstone of the whole edifice", but the Chiefs of Staff Committee had become the power plant'.

Subordinate to the Chiefs of Staff Committee were the Joint Planning Committee, appointed in 1927, the Deputy Chiefs of Staff Committee, set up in 1932, and the Joint Intelligence Committee, created in 1936. The Joint Planning Committee consisted of the Directors of Plans of the three services. Whenever a strategic problem was placed before the CID, the Joint Planning Committee, working as a team, would prepare an outline plan to meet the situation, and this plan would then be passed to the Chiefs of Staff and the full CID for further refinement before final submission to the Cabinet. The Joint Intelligence Committee's task was to provide accurate and up-to-date information on any problems under consideration. It was chaired by a representative of the Foreign Office and included the three service Directors of Intelligence. All these bodies were served by the CID secretariat.

THE MENACE OF THE BOMBER

During the First World War aircraft had added a new dimension to warfare. With the advent of the bomber, civilians at home were no longer immune from attack. Between 1914 and 1918 some 300 tons of bombs were dropped on Britain, causing 4,820 casualties, of which 1,413 were fatal. The threat posed by the bomber led the CID, in 1924, to appoint an Air Raid Precautions Sub-Committee under Sir John Anderson, then Permanent Under-Secretary of the Home Office. One of this Committee's priorities was to consider the question of the location of the seat of government in a future war, given that London was expected to be subjected to heavy bombing at the very start of such a conflict. By mid-1924 the Air Staff estimated that an enemy air force would seek to inflict a knock-out blow on London by dropping 200 tons of bombs on the capital in the first twenty-four hours, causing 5,000 casualties, and that the attack might be sustained, albeit at a reduced level, for at least a month. After analysing these estimates, the ARP Committee concluded that the adverse effects on civilian morale which would result from moving the seat of government out of London outweighed the advantages of evacuation. However, they recommended that the Office of Works should produce contingency plans for both the partial and total evacuation of Whitehall in case either course proved necessary.

15

Partly because of the continued acceptance of the 'ten-year rule', no real progress was made in this matter during the next decade and none of the evacuation schemes proposed in 1925 were in fact prepared. But, in 1933, the situation was radically altered by the rise to power in Germany of Adolf Hitler. In October 1933 Germany withdrew from the Disarmament Conference at Geneva and declared her intention to leave the League of Nations. Early the following year, the Committee of Imperial Defence recognised Germany as the potential enemy for the purposes of long-term defence planning and in July 1934 the Government announced a five-year programme for the expansion of the RAF. The official birth of the Luftwaffe and the reintroduction of conscription in Germany in 1935 forced Britain to increase the scale and tempo of her own rearmament. In March 1936 the Government introduced a Defence White Paper, embodying what was described in the Commons by Neville Chamberlain, the Chancellor of the Exchequer, as 'the largest programme of defence ever undertaken by this country in peacetime'. In order to take some of the load of responsibility for defence off the shoulders of the Prime Minister, Stanley Baldwin, the post of Minister for the Co-ordination of Defence was created. The new minister was to exercise, on the Prime Minister's behalf, the day-to-day supervision of the CID and could convene the Chiefs of Staff under his own chairmanship, but he had no depart-

ment and no executive authority. Many expected Churchill to be given the post, yet Baldwin surprisingly chose Sir Thomas Inskip, the Attorney General, who had little experience of defence problems.

The Defence White Paper of March 1936 also announced the strengthening of the Joint Planning Committee, each of the Directors of Plans being provided with a deputy who would be employed full-time on combined planning work. The same year, Colonel H L Ismay, who had served as an Assistant Secretary from 1925 to 1930, was appointed Deputy Secretary of the CID, and Major L C Hollis was brought in as an additional Assistant Secretary to handle the business of the reinforced Joint Planning Committee. Both men were to play a central role in the story of the Cabinet War Rooms.

PLANNING FOR THE PROTECTION OF GOVERNMENT ▪▪

As part of Britain's preparations for a possible war with Germany, the Committee of Imperial Defence paid renewed attention to the safety of the higher organs of control. In February 1936 it appointed a special Sub-Committee on the Location of Government Staffs on the Outbreak of War, chaired by Sir Warren Fisher, the Permanent Secretary to the Treasury, and during the summer the Cabinet approved a plan for a new Government building on the Whitehall Gardens site, incorporating a gas and splinter-proof basement. All planning was coloured by the latest Air Staff calculations on the likely scale of attack. It was now estimated that over 600 tons of bombs per day might be dropped on Britain in the first few weeks of a war, indicating casualties in the order of 200,000 a week, of whom 66,000 would be killed. The Warren Fisher Committee therefore recommended 'the principle of dispersion' of the Government machine, which included earmarking alternative shelter accommodation in the London suburbs for the most essential departments. In February 1937 the Cabinet authorised the formation of yet another committee, headed by Sir James Rae, an Under-Secretary at the Treasury, to turn these principles into a comprehensive scheme.

The Rae Committee, which presented its initial report in October 1937, also favoured evacuation. The report identified some 12,000 officials as being essential to the prosecution of the war, categorising them as 'Group A' staffs; others were classed as 'non-essentials' and constituted 'Group B'. In an emergency, Group A staffs should go first to schools and other public buildings in the north-west suburbs of London and, if these were found to be vulnerable, they would then move to locations in the West Country. The Rae Com-

ABOVE Major-General Sir Hastings (later General Lord) Ismay. Born in 1887, Ismay, who was known as 'Pug' to his colleagues and friends, served as an officer in the Indian Army and had been seconded to the Committee of Imperial Defence between 1925 and 1930. He became its Secretary and Deputy Secretary (Military) to the Cabinet on Hankey's retirement in 1938. In 1940, he was appointed Chief of Staff to Churchill in the latter's capacity as Minister of Defence and thereafter sat on the Chiefs of Staff Committee as well as retaining his post as Deputy Secretary (Military) to the War Cabinet. For much of the Second World War he acted as the link between Churchill and the Chiefs of Staff and the tact and skill with which he performed his demanding duties were key factors in securing the firm and steady direction from the top on which the success of Britain's war effort depended. Ismay was promoted Lieutenant-General in 1942 and full General in 1944, and was created a Baron in 1947. He died in 1965. *IWM HU 44792*

ABOVE Adolf Hitler speaking at a Nazi Party rally in Germany in the mid-1930s. German rearmament under Hitler and, in particular, the rapid rebuilding of the German air force, caused increasing concern about the safety of the central organs of government in Britain in the event of a future war. *IWM MH 10456*

mittee commented on the need for each of the services to have a secure 'nerve centre', close enough to each other to ensure adequate liaison, and called for the construction of War Rooms, proof against hits by 500 lb semi-armour-piercing bombs, in Cricklewood, Harrow and Dollis Hill. Hankey himself observed at this time that the ideal arrangement would be to have a 'National GHQ' building to house the Cabinet, the Chiefs of Staff and other important bodies. Meanwhile the Office of Works began to survey existing Government buildings and to make plans for the structural protection of new ones such as the projected block in Whitehall Gardens.

PROPOSALS FOR A 'CENTRAL WAR ROOM'

On 14 December 1937, the Deputy Chiefs of Staff, swayed by the confusion evident in recent air defence exercises, echoed the demands for some sort of nerve centre to guarantee satisfactory inter-service co-ordination, urging that, if war came, the Chiefs of Staff, Deputy Chiefs of Staff and Joint Planners should all be housed in a 'Central War Room'. This would include a map room where the Chiefs of Staff could confer every day and where their decisions would be transformed into orders on the spot by the Deputy Chiefs of Staff. Early in March 1938 the Air Ministry submitted an elaborate scheme for a purpose-built, underground 'Combined War Room', resembling Hankey's idea of the previous October. While the plan was being studied, the German invasion and annexation of Austria during the second week of March gave the matter fresh urgency. Accordingly, on 16 March, Ismay instructed the Office of Works to explore the possibilities of providing an emergency working refuge for the Cabinet and Chiefs of Staff as a safeguard against sudden attack. Hitherto, the Cabinet Office had assumed that a Central War Room could be established in the cellars of the new Whitehall building but now acknowledged that this would not be ready for four years. The Cabinet Office and CID therefore accepted that a temporary War Room, designed to fit into any suitable basement which became available, might have to be used, particularly if hostilities commenced before the more ambitious plans for a 'Combined War Room' could be realised.

Late in March the Deputy Chiefs of Staff re-emphasised the need for a Central War Room where the Chiefs of Staff could be supplied with properly correlated intelligence, adding that the site must be protected against bombs and gas. Ordered by the Chiefs of Staff on 4 April to prepare a scheme for the layout and organisation of the proposed emergency war headquarters the Deputy Chiefs of Staff produced a memorandum eighteen days later in which the functions of the Central War Room were more sharply defined. It was seen mainly as a focal point for the collation of intelligence and the co-ordination of operations, tasks to be performed by the Chiefs and Deputy Chiefs of Staff, the Joint Planning Committee and the Joint Intelligence Committee. The War Room, in their view, should incorporate conference facilities, a map room open twenty-four hours a day, safe communications to other command centres, and domestic offices for the occupants. The Deputy Chiefs of Staff conceded that fully-integrated headquarters would be required for the actual conduct of certain types of operations, like air defence and coastal defence, but did not believe that the Central War Room should be used in this way. Although the Chiefs of Staff and their deputies would confer there, it would still be left to the respective service staffs to convert their decisions into operational orders. Thus the Central War Room was not to serve as an operational headquarters, neither was it intended to replace the individual service War Rooms.

THE SITE IS SELECTED

A t a meeting on 4 May 1938 the CID agreed that provision should be made to house the Cabinet as well as the Chiefs of Staff in a Central War Room. The Deputy Chiefs of Staff had barely begun to embody this extra requirement in their working plan when German troop movements on the frontiers of Czechoslovakia led the Czech government to order a partial mobilisation on 21 May and for a few days war seemed imminent. Ismay immediately obtained informal approval for the preparation of a 'Central Emergency Headquarters' and issued appropriate orders to the Office of Works. The latter carried out a rapid survey of available basements in London and concluded that the most suitable rooms were those under the western side of the New Public Offices, the huge building bounded by Whitehall, Great George Street, Storey's Gate and Horse Guards Road, and King Charles Street. Built between 1898 and 1915, the New Public Offices had a steel-framed structure and so offered better protection against the effects of bombing than older Government buildings in Whitehall. Moreover, the block was conveniently close to Downing Street, Whitehall Gardens and the principal ministries. The western side of the building, facing St James's Park, then housed the Office of Works itself.

Towards the end of May Ismay was formally made responsible for the Central War Room and Commander Angus Nicholl, the Naval Assistant Secretary to the CID, was sent to inspect the rooms in the Office of Works basement. The rooms were some ten feet below ground level and were being used by the Office of Works for the storage of archives. On 31 May Nicholl reported that the New Pub-

ABOVE Major-General (later General Sir) Leslie Hollis, photographed in the Map Room of the Cabinet War Room in 1945. Hollis, who was born in 1897, served as an officer in the Royal Marines prior to his appointment as an Assistant Secretary of the Committee of Imperial Defence in 1936. He played a leading part in the establishment of the original 'Central War Room' in the basement under the New Public Offices in the years immediately before the Second World War and took over as Secretary to the Chiefs of Staff Committee when Major-General Ismay became Chief of Staff to Churchill as Minister of Defence in 1940. As Senior Assistant Secretary (Military) to the War Cabinet he remained closely involved with the Cabinet War Room throughout the war. He was promoted full General in 1951 and died in 1963. *(Paul Popper)*

ABOVE Lawrence Burgis in the Map Room of the Cabinet War Room which he helped to set up in 1938 and 1939. During these years Burgis was also responsible for putting the finishing touches to the War Book, the blueprint for the actions to be taken by the various elements of the Government when war appeared to be imminent. Burgis, who was born in 1892, served as Assistant Secretary to the War Cabinet in 1918, as Private Secretary to Sir Maurice Hankey from 1921 to 1937 and again as Assistant Secretary to the War Cabinet from 1939 to 1945. Burgis acted as Camp Commandant of the Cabinet War Room between 1943 and 1945. He died in 1972. *(Paul Popper)* lic Offices block was the strongest in Whitehall and that the basement rooms, which could be cleared of their contents and protected easily and unobtrusively, offered the safest accommodation available at short notice. The CID secretariat agreed that the rooms were indeed suitable for emergency use and accepted them that very day. The recruitment of staff was at once put in hand and a number of retired officers were quietly approached and designated for future duty as mapkeepers.

The following week the Chiefs of Staff gave Ismay a free hand to supervise the project and on 10 June he delegated the task to Hollis, who was to be assisted by Eric de Normann, an Assistant Secretary in the Office of Works, and Lawrence Burgis, an experienced member of the Cabinet Office and Hankey's Private Secretary from 1921 to 1937. A sub-committee of the Joint Planning Committee was formed to advise on the scheme. Ismay and Hollis knew they had to allow space for the Cabinet and its secretariat in the Central War Room, but the idea that the Chiefs of Staff might plan operations there, as opposed to using the War Room merely to coordinate plans already made, was now growing. Since the Chiefs of Staff, in this situation, would require the presence of the Joint Planners, it was confirmed that the latter would have to be housed permanently in the War Room. In endorsing these arrangements, the Joint Planners' sub-committee moved that the emergency headquarters should be fitted out as soon as possible. 'Nothing very elaborate is contemplated; no major structural alterations, no air-conditioning or costly gas proofing, and no expensive fittings', Ismay informed the Treasury on 18 June, showing that, at this juncture, the use of the Office of Works basement was still seen as a purely temporary expedient pending the provision of permanent accommodation elsewhere.

THE CENTRAL WAR ROOM TAKES SHAPE

Two days before Ismay wrote to the Treasury, de Normann gave instructions for the clearance of several rooms in the basement. Rooms 62 to 65A, which flanked the middle and northern sections of the main corridor in the western basement area of the New Public Offices, were empty by 25 June and Room 61A, off the southern half of the corridor, was vacated on 29 June. The most northerly of these rooms, 65A, was allocated for use by the Cabinet while Room 64, slightly to the south, was picked as a meeting-place for the Chiefs of Staff. A larger room between the two – Room 65 – was to become the Map Room.

During this period a fourth person joined Hollis and his team. He was George Rance, an Office of Works official who was then less than a year away from retirement. Besides being in charge of the pay sheets of cleaning staff in the Office of Works, Rance was also responsible for ordering furniture and thus, when asked to clear the basement rooms and fit them out with tables, chairs and other items, he was able to do so without attracting unwanted attention. Furniture, maps and documents intended for the Central War Room were addressed simply 'c/o Mr Rance, Office of Works, Whitehall' in order to maintain the secrecy of the project.

With the Central War Room at last taking shape, it was imperative for it to have a secure communications system. The special sub-committee of the Joint Planning Committee urged in mid-June that the Post Office should install twelve direct telephone lines at the earliest opportunity. On 17 June Hollis approved a GPO plan to colour-code the telephones. White telephones would be used for direct lines to other War Rooms, green for direct lines to intelligence sources and black for lines to the official private branch exchange. It was decided to put in eight direct lines to the Map Room and four for the Chiefs of Staff or the Joint Planners in Room 64. Seven black telephones would also be placed in the basement. Over the next few years, the system was greatly enlarged and considerably modified to conform with the expansion of the complex as a whole and with changes in the use of certain rooms.

By mid-summer the Chiefs of Staff and Hankey were swinging towards the belief that the principal elements of government should stay in London as long as possible. In the first week of July 1938, steps were taken to sound-proof the Map Room (65) and the rooms for the Chiefs of Staff and Cabinet (64 and 65A), and to build brick partitions in some of the larger cellars. On 9 July Hollis issued further instructions relating to the Map Room. The chief task of the officers manning this room would be to collate and summarise all relevant information on the progress of the war and present it on maps, which would be constantly up-dated for the benefit of the Chiefs of Staff. The Map Room was to remain open day and night. The Office of Works arranged to cover the walls with compressed fibre-board suitable for mounting maps and to supply standard desks and chairs for the occupants. Structural alterations too were pushed through with some speed. Alcoves in the wall along the St James's Park side of the basement were sandbagged, glass doors were replaced with teak ones and a number of other doors were bricked up to seal off the corridor. Plans were also laid to provide air locks, with steel doors, at the entrances in case of gas attack.

Having served for more than a quarter of a century as Secretary of the CID and for over twenty years as Secretary to the Cabinet, Hankey retired at the end of July 1938. Neville Chamberlain, now the Prime Minister, had come to the conclusion that Hankey's dual role was fast becoming too big for one person to perform and so decided to separate the two appointments. For the post of Permanent Secretary of the Cabinet Office and Secretary to the Cabinet he chose Edward Bridges, who for some time had been head of the division of the Treasury dealing with the financial aspects of defence policy. Ismay was appointed Deputy Secretary (Military) to the Cabinet and Secretary of the CID, while Sir Rupert Howorth continued as Deputy Secretary (Civil) to the Cabinet. These changes did not slow down the work on the War Room complex which, in August, expanded southwards along the basement corridor into Rooms 60, 60A and 61, previously used for the storage of records by the Board of Trade, then occupying the Great George Street side of the building. The same month the site was fitted for broadcasting. The BBC agreed to supply two sets of outside broadcast equipment, circuits were connected to Broadcasting House and Maida Vale, and the emergency Cabinet Room (65A) was wired for a microphone and lined with boards to improve its acoustics. The Map Room was manned and tested before the end of August.

THE MUNICH CRISIS

Any lingering doubts about the wisdom of creating a refuge for the higher organs of government and command were dispelled in late August and early September 1938 when a new European crisis was precipitated by Hitler's threat to annex the Sudeten region of Czechoslovakia, which contained some three million ethnic Germans. While Chamberlain sought to defuse the crisis by diplomatic means, culminating in the Munich Agreement of 30 September, whereby the Czechs were compelled to cede the Sudetenland to Germany, the preparation of the War Room gained momentum. By 14 September the situation was serious enough for Ismay to declare that a mechanical ventilation system for the basement, an installation so far accorded a relatively low priority by the Office of Works, might well be needed within a week. In the next few days the Office of Works, under pressure to make the rooms fit for immediate occupation, ordered a gas filter and the wiring necessary for auxiliary lighting. As the crisis approached its peak in the last week of September, the ventilation system was rigged up and operated by Office of Works engineers, though the overhead metal ducts, which had adjustable nozzles to enable the flow of air to be altered or cut off altogether, were as yet only fitted in the three main rooms towards the northern end of the basement. Other staff worked hard to shore up the roofs of these three rooms with crude timber props and beams which were braced together as a precaution against the

FACING PAGE TOP Sir Edward (later Lord) Bridges, Secretary to the Cabinet from 1938 to 1939 and 1945 to 1946, and Secretary to the War Cabinet from 1939 to 1945. Bridges was born in 1892 and was the son of Robert Bridges, the Poet Laureate. He had a distinguished career at the Treasury before succeeding Hankey as Secretary to the Cabinet in 1938. His relations with Churchill, when the latter became Prime Minister in 1940, were at first somewhat uneasy but Churchill later came to describe him as 'a man of exceptional force, ability and personal charm'. Although he was recognised as the head of the War Cabinet Secretariat, he left the military aspects of its business largely to Ismay and concentrated on ensuring that the civil aspects were not overlooked and that matters for decision were brought forward at the right point in the War Cabinet machine. He was therefore, in effect, Churchill's chief civilian staff officer. Bridges died in 1969. *Courtesy of the Cabinet Office*

FACING PAGE BELOW Major-General Hollis and Lawrence Burgis in the Map Room of the Cabinet War Room. Although this picture was taken after the end of the war in Europe, it clearly shows the crude timber props and beams installed in the Map Room at the time of the Munich crisis in September 1938. These were intended to help shore up the ceiling of the room as a precaution against the possible collapse of the building above during an air raid. *IWM HU 43547*

ABOVE Neville Chamberlain at Heston Airport on 30 September 1938, a few hours after his meeting with Hitler in Munich. Chamberlain is waving a document, signed by Hitler and himself, in which the two leaders had expressed their determination 'to remove possible sources of difference and thus to contribute to assure the peace of Europe'. Less than a year later Britain was at war with Germany. The document which Chamberlain is holding in this photograph is now on display in the Imperial War Museum. *IWM D 2239* possible collapse of the building above during an air raid. Even if the facilities were incomplete, Hollis thought that they were adequate for emergency use and, from 26 September, he carried the keys of the War Room with him in case they were required in a hurry.

The Central War Room had quickly outgrown the simple and inexpensive refuge envisaged by Ismay four months earlier, but as the danger of war temporarily receded following the Munich Agreement the basement was closed and placed on a care and maintenance footing. Hollis used the respite to analyse the faults revealed by the manning of the War Room during the Munich crisis and reported them to Ismay on 3 November. Hollis complained that the air in the Map Room became unpleasant after several hours of occupation, felt that the washing facilities were poor and suggested that a stock of bedding and reserves of food should be supplied for staff who might be forced to stay in the basement for prolonged periods because of bombing or the pressure of work. Another obvious requirement was for the War Room to have its own telephone switchboard. Hollis advised that service personnel rather than Office of Works charladies should be employed as cleaners and, shortly afterwards, a detachment of ten Royal Marine pensioners, including two corporals, was organised to act as guards and general orderlies. In December Ismay arranged with the Office of Works for the roof of the basement to be reinforced with steel girders and for Room 60, near the southern end of the corridor, to be strutted with timber props and beams and partitioned so that it could house a switchboard.

If the weight of official opinion had shifted in favour of remaining in protected accommodation in London and against evacuation, no final decision had yet been taken and work on the proposed War Rooms in the suburbs went on side by side with that in Whitehall. One of the suburban citadels, code-named 'Paddock', which was to be built under the Post Office Research Station at Dollis Hill, was intended as an alternative headquarters for the Cabinet and Chiefs of Staff and was to have similar facilities and communications to those at Storey's Gate. The Committee of Imperial Defence realised that this, and the other suburban citadels, would take some time to complete so, in the interim, the Office of Works was asked to concentrate on providing the maximum amount of protected accommodation in central London for short-term use. The Office of Works understandably objected to the duplication of effort and resources involved in all these plans and suggested in January 1939 that, if central London became uninhabitable, essential staffs should go straight to the West Country and not initially to the suburbs, thus avoiding a double move. The Cabinet subsequently accepted this advice and work on the suburban War Rooms was given a lower priority, though not abandoned.

THE APPROACH OF WAR

To date, the Central War Room had been developed largely as a result of decisions made by the CID secretariat without much guidance from above. Early in January 1939 the Deputy Chiefs of Staff therefore requested some clarification of the role of the emergency war headquarters. The new Minister for the Co-ordination of Defence, Admiral of the Fleet Lord Chatfield, who succeeded Inskip that month, confirmed that it should function as a centre in which the Cabinet and Chiefs of Staff, helped by the Joint Planning and Joint Intelligence Committees, could make and co-ordinate plans, and he repeated that it should not be used as an operational headquarters. However, Chatfield also touched on the need for overnight accommodation for those who would be working there. The problem of finding such additional space in or near the basement preoccupied Hollis in the months ahead and generated some conflict between the CID and the Office of Works.

On 11 January 1939 the Office of Works told Hollis that dormitories could be set up in two rooms next to the main staircase on the sub-ground floor of the New Public Offices, immediately above the basement. Hollis also began to investigate the possibility of utilising space in the sub-basement, known as the 'Dock', beneath the Central War Room. Later in the month, the plan to provide domestic accommodation suffered a setback when the Office of Works insisted that work on the dormitories must be deferred. Because the original understanding had been that the War Room would be fitted into the basement as it stood, without major changes, the Office of Works was experiencing difficulties in coping with the stream of demands for rooms and structural alterations that the development of the War Room was creating. A further exercise to test the Map Room and its mapkeepers was held in mid-February, demonstrating that at least three shifts of mapkeepers would be necessary to man the room over a twenty-four hour cycle, and on 23 March the Office of Works was able to report that all the rooms so far selected had now been strutted with timber props and beams.

The time available for additional improvements was, in fact, rapidly running out. On 15 March German troops occupied the remainder of Czechoslovakia; on the last day of the month Britain pledged support to Poland in the event of any act which endangered Polish independence; and on 28 April Hitler renounced the 1934 Non-Aggression Treaty between Germany and Poland. The accelerating pace of the slide towards war was reflected in the preparations at Storey's Gate. The mapkeepers were placed under orders to go to the Central War Room on their own initiative if a sudden crisis arose and by the beginning of April most of the maps likely to be needed at the outbreak of war were mounted and ready for use. Three

weeks later Burgis informed the BBC that the southernmost half of the recently-partitioned Room 60 would be allocated to them as a small office. The outside broadcast equipment was locked away in a steel cabinet until required.

The lack of progress in the matter of dormitories led the Deputy Chiefs of Staff, at the end of June, to observe that immediate changes were necessary if the War Room was to be at instant readiness to function under any foreseeable conditions. They supported a plea by Hollis for sleeping accommodation for an estimated thirty overnight users and recommended that proper lavatories should be substituted for the primitive arrangements then obtaining, which consisted mainly of a row of buckets in the corridor of the sub-basement. Those in need should not be expected to climb three flights of stairs to the conveniences on the first floor of the building during an air raid. Equally, air raids might prevent staff from eating in the Office of Works restaurant on the ground floor, so the basement should be equipped with a kitchen and reserves of food and water. An officer of the CID secretariat would be appointed as 'Camp Commandant' to supervise the domestic services of the Central War Room.

Hollis noted on 17 July that the ventilation system was at last fully operational, yet the accommodation question continued to worry him throughout the summer. He calculated that if the basement was used only once in a while for specific meetings of the Cabinet and its committees, essential services could be performed by a nucleus staff of 39, but he forecast that a staff of 46 people would be needed for anything more regular and that as many as 120 might be present on occasion. As it was, some of the typists would have to work in the corridor when the basement rooms were fully occupied. The problem of feeding, however, was solved by a compromise. Meals would be provided by the Office of Works restaurant when possible; otherwise, orderlies on the War Room staff would prepare snacks. Provision was also made for the War Office to supply standard rations sufficient to feed 75 people for three days in an emergency.

After a familiarisation exercise for the staff early in August, the Committee of Imperial Defence returned to the problem of domestic accommodation. At a meeting held in the Central War Room on 22 August the CID concluded that the two rooms earmarked on the sub-ground floor must be used as men's and women's dormitories, with twelve and ten beds respectively. Chemical toilets were to be placed behind partitions near the stairs to the St James's Park entrance. In the basement itself, Room 68, until now a mess room for Office of Works coal porters, would offer space for a snack bar where simple meals and drinks could be prepared for the staff of the War Room. It was decided that, as the basement was already stretched to the limit, the sub-basement would probably have to be used for accommodation, even though it had very low headroom and was cluttered with pipes and ducts. The Office of Works accepted the proposals on 24 August. The coal porters were turned out of Room 68 and the dormitory rooms on the sub-ground floor were finally handed over. The Admiralty was asked to release Captain B F Adams so that he could take up his appointment as Camp Commandant.

War was now less than a fortnight away. On 23 August the world was shaken by the news that Germany and Russia had signed a Non-Aggression Pact, leaving Hitler free to attack Poland without fear of retaliation from the Soviet Union. In Britain the Government set in motion the well-laid plans and procedures outlined in the War Book, which had been duly revised by the CID during the past two decades. The Central War Room was opened up on Sunday 27 August 1939 and the mapkeepers, called up from their civilian occupations, began their first watch in the Map Room that afternoon. Six years would elapse before the Map Room lights were switched off again.

CHAMBERLAIN'S WAR CABINET

On 1 September 1939 Chamberlain informed the Cabinet of his intention 'to set up a War Cabinet at once on the model of that established in the last war'. It had been expected that the War Cabinet would contain six members, mostly without normal departmental duties, but when it met for the first time on 3 September, five hours after the declaration of war, it numbered nine, including Chamberlain. Those with departmental duties were Sir John Simon, the Chancellor of the Exchequer; Lord Halifax, the Foreign Secretary; Leslie Hore-Belisha, the Secretary of State for War; Sir Kingsley Wood, the Secretary of State for Air; and Winston Churchill, now First Lord of the Admiralty. The members with no departmental responsibilities were Sir Samuel Hoare, the Lord Privy Seal; Lord Chatfield, the Minister for the Co-ordination of Defence; and Hankey, who had been elevated to the peerage that year, as Minister without Portfolio. Because Chamberlain was anxious for Churchill to join this team after ten years out of office, the latter's appointment to the Admiralty and membership of the War Cabinet made it logical to include the other service ministers as well, thus giving a larger number than originally contemplated.

The secretariats of the Cabinet and the Committee of Imperial Defence were merged into a single body, known as the War Cabinet Secretariat. The Committee of Imperial Defence ceased to have

ABOVE Chamberlain's War Cabinet in 1939. In the back row, reading from left to right, are: Sir Kingsley Wood (Secretary of State for Air); Winston Churchill (First Lord of the Admiralty); Leslie Hore-Belisha (Secretary of State for War); and Lord Hankey (Minister without Portfolio). Seated in front, from left to right, are: Lord Halifax (Foreign Secretary); Sir John Simon (Chancellor of the Exchequer); Neville Chamberlain (Prime Minister); Sir Samuel Hoare (Lord Privy Seal); and Lord Chatfield (Minister for the Co-ordination of Defence). *Radio Times Hulton Picture Library*

ABOVE The underground Cabinet Room (Room 69). Chamberlain's War Cabinet met here only once, in October 1939, but under Churchill more than one hundred meetings of the War Cabinet were held in this room between 1940 and 1945. Churchill himself sat in the large wooden chair in front of the map on the left of this picture. At meetings of the Defence Committee (Operations), the Chiefs of Staff occupied the places immediately facing Churchill inside the hollow square formed by the tables. Note the metal ventilation duct which was installed in the room in the autumn of 1939. *IWM MH 524*

a separate existence on 5 September and was never resurrected. Bridges stayed at the head of the structure as Secretary to the War Cabinet and, together with Howorth as Deputy Secretary (Civil), handled the civil aspects of War Cabinet business. Ismay as Deputy Secretary (Military), helped by Hollis as Senior Assistant Secretary (Military), dealt with the military side. Each wing of the War Cabinet Secretariat contained eight or more Assistant Secretaries. Hankey's influence remained strong in the military wing for apart from Ismay and Hollis at least one of the Assistant Secretaries, Lieutenant-Colonel E I C Jacob, had been hand-picked by him before his retirement. Although the volume of work and the speed with which it was conducted significantly increased, there was no basic change in the organisation of the War Cabinet Secretariat as a committee machine, and the methods employed for the distribution of papers, the arrangement of meetings and the circulation of conclusions followed the pattern which had evolved in the previous twenty years.

Once the CID had disappeared, the Chiefs of Staff began to report direct to the War Cabinet. Without the CID to act as a filter, the War Cabinet found itself involved in the formulation of military policy in too much detail and at too early a stage. It was therefore felt that there should be some smaller ministerial body which could concentrate on defence matters and form a link between the War Cabinet and the Chiefs of Staff Committee. To fill this gap, a Standing Ministerial Committee on Military Co-ordination was appointed in October 1939, comprising Chatfield as chairman, the three service ministers, and Leslie Burgin, the Minister of Supply. Its terms of reference were 'to keep under constant review on behalf of the War Cabinet the main factors in the strategical situation and the progress of operations, and to make recommendations from time to time to the War Cabinet as to the general conduct of the war'.

THE DEVELOPMENT OF THE WAR ROOM, ■■■■■■■
SEPTEMBER 1939 – MAY 1940 ■■■■■■■■■■■

C ontrary to pre-war predictions, the anticipated air attacks on London did not materialise in September 1939. Nevertheless, work on the protected accommodation below the New Public Offices proceeded without a pause. Ismay particularly wanted to find a larger area than Room 65A for the War Cabinet. Captain A N Barnard of the War Cabinet Secretariat advised him on 5 September that the only suitable room was Room 69, an Office of Works refuge at the northern end of the basement corridor, which had been intended as a shelter for 80 people. The Office of Works reluctantly agreed to sacrifice this area and in mid-September Room 69 was fitted with a teak door and its external walls were sandbagged. Room 68, at the north-western corner of the corridor, which was to serve as a waiting room and mess, was also sandbagged and given a new, stronger door. The Joint Planners took over Room 65A and also occupied Room 62A. Further south, the rooms allocated to Ismay and Bridges, 61 and 61A, were partitioned to provide office accommodation for their respective assistants. Room 60A and the northern half of Room 60 were allocated to typists. Somehow space was found in the latter for a small War Cabinet Office switchboard, while the southern half of Room 60 continued to house the BBC equipment. In spite of this reorganisation, there was no let-up in the calls for rooms, especially for the Joint Planning Committee staff which was increasing in size to meet wartime requirements. As it was vital for the Joint Planners to remain close to the Map Room they tended, in the coming months, to occupy any room which became temporarily vacant.

By 4 October the ventilation system had been extended to Room 69 and the room was ready for use by the War Cabinet, thus completing the first major phase of expansion of the War Room, which retained much the same physical form and layout until more radical demands were made upon its capacity in the summer of 1940. The War Cabinet held its first meeting in Room 69 on 21 October 1939, partly to test the facilities, but did not return to the basement to meet as a body that year. However, ministers did visit the Map Room to keep abreast of the latest military situation. During this period, the Map Room was normally manned by one mapkeeper from each service, with a fourth acting as Duty Officer. There were four watches in every twenty-four hour cycle, with the first beginning at 11 pm, the second at 6 am, the third at 12.30 pm, and the last at 6.30 pm. Each service had a pool of some six mapkeepers who worked on a rota system. The Map Room staff gathered information from the service War Rooms, plotted it, then passed on important items of news, via Ismay and Hollis, to the Joint Planners, to Buckingham Palace and to the Cabinet Office, which had moved to Richmond Terrace in 1938. The mapkeepers were required to prepare a summary for the Chiefs of Staff by 9 am each day and helped the Joint Planners, who frequently worked in the Map Room, with the writing of reports and appreciations. In October 1939 only 46 persons were allowed unrestricted access to the Map Room. They included the War Cabinet, the Chiefs and Deputy Chiefs of Staff, the Joint Planning Committee and thirteen members of the War Cabinet Secretariat.

On 29 December 1939 the name of the basement headquarters was officially changed to the 'Cabinet War Room' and its functions were defined by Bridges as being to supply current, fully-correlated information about the war in all parts of the world for the War Cabinet,

the Chiefs of Staff and the King, and to provide a protected meeting-place for the War Cabinet and Chiefs of Staff during air raids. By the spring of 1940 the Cabinet War Room was in reasonable working order. It had expanded from a nucleus of three rooms to a suite of at least sixteen, with working and living accommodation for 60 people. The Map Room was running smoothly and the communications to other key centres were operational. The War Room was still hardly used by the War Cabinet, so although the basement was over-crowded, it was able to fulfil most of the tasks laid down for it by Bridges.

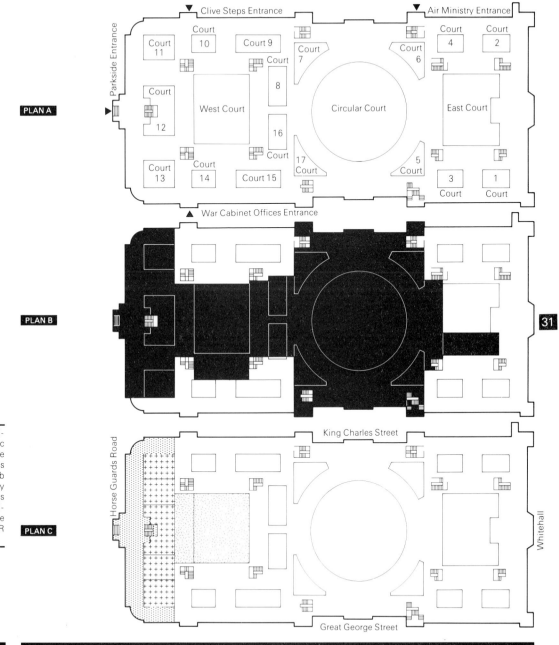

PLAN A

▼ Clive Steps Entrance   ▼ Air Ministry Entrance

Parkside Entrance

Court 11   Court 10   Court 9   Court 7   Court 6   Court 4   Court 2

Court 8

West Court   Circular Court   East Court

Court 12

Court 16

Court 13   Court 14   Court 15   Court 17   Court 5   Court 3   Court 1

▲ War Cabinet Offices Entrance

PLAN B

PLAN C

Horse Guards Road

King Charles Street

Whitehall

Great George Street

RIGHT Plan of the Government Offices, Great George Street (New Public Offices), showing (A) the location of the inner courtyards; (B) the basement areas covered by the reinforced concrete slab by the summer of 1942 (indicated by shading); and (C) the respective areas occupied, at basement level, by the original Cabinet War Room complex, the Courtyard Rooms and the 'CWR Annexe'.

KEY TO PLAN C

▨ Original War Room Area

+++ Courtyard Rooms

▧ 'CWR Annexe'

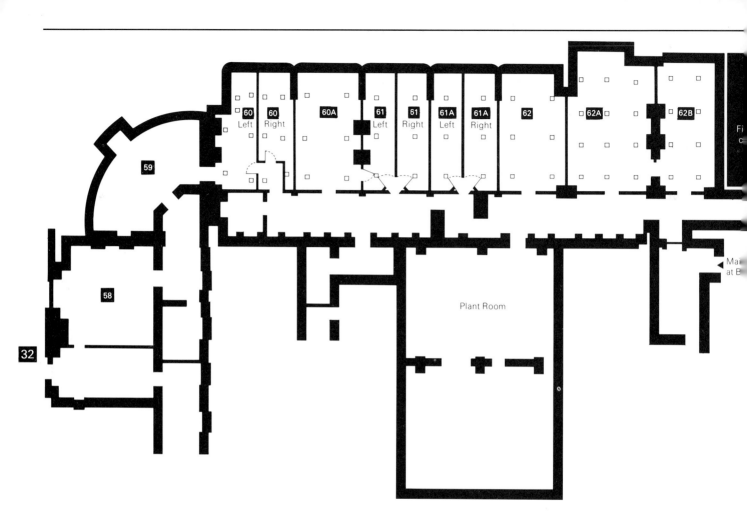

Plan of the western basement of the Government Offices, Great George Street (New Public Offices), showing the location of the various rooms which together formed the nucleus of the original Cabinet War Room complex between 1938 and 1945.

0 1 2 3 4 5 6 7 8 9 10

Scale in metres

N →

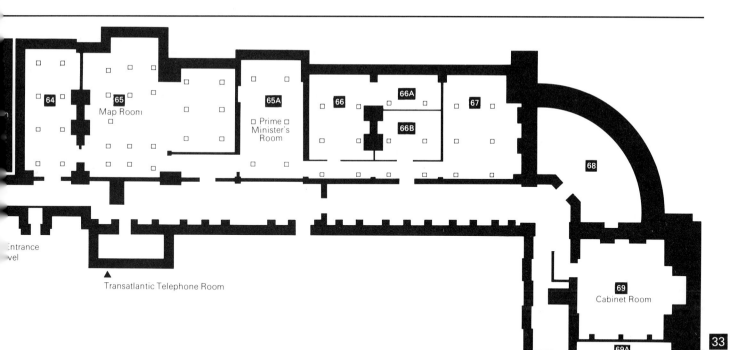

64

65
Map Room

65A

Prime
Minister's
Room

66

66A

66B

67

68

Entrance
vel

▲
Transatlantic Telephone Room

69
Cabinet Room

69A

33

BELOW Elevation of the western, or St James's Park, side of the Government Offices, Great George Street, formerly known as the New Public Offices. The numbers in the ground-floor windows indicate the various rooms occupied by the 'No. 10 Annexe'. The other numbers indicate the respective levels of the reinforced concrete slab, the basement housing the Cabinet War Rooms, and the sub-basement or 'Dock'.

34

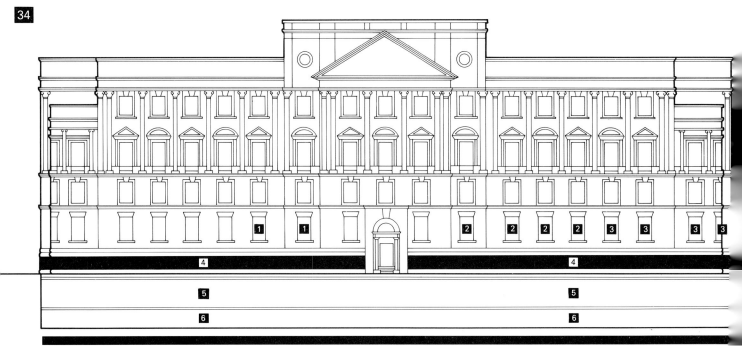

Even during the lull of the 'Phoney War' period in the winter of 1939–40, faults were apparent in the system of supreme direction. Chamberlain saw to it that Cabinet meetings were conducted in an orderly fashion but was out of his depth in military matters and lacked the drive to ensure that Britain would gain every possible advantage from the breathing-space granted to her. The Chiefs of Staff, after detailed discussion of a problem, would report to the Ministerial Committee on Military Co-ordination. There the same ground was covered all over again before the matter was placed before the War Cabinet and the whole process of explanation and discussion would then be repeated. The Military Co-ordination Committee proved unsatisfactory, for Chatfield, its chairman, had no executive power and Churchill, with his energy, eloquence and long study of war, tended to dominate its meetings. Sir Ian Jacob, then Military Assistant Secretary to the War Cabinet, later recalled that 'Churchill was so much larger in every way than his colleagues on this Committee that it ran like a coach with one wheel twice the size of the other three, and achieved very little with much friction'.

Chatfield resigned on 3 April 1940 and Chamberlain's own position was undermined by the disasters of the campaign in Norway in the month that followed. When Germany attacked the Low Countries on 10 May he too resigned and Churchill succeeded him as Prime Minister that evening. Churchill at once formed a coalition government with a War Cabinet of five, including Chamberlain as Lord President of the Council, Halifax as Foreign Secretary and, from the Labour Party, Clement Attlee as Lord Privy Seal and Arthur Greenwood as Minister without Portfolio. The three service ministers were excluded. Before the end of 1940 the membership had grown to eight with the admission of Lord Beaverbrook as Minister of Aircraft Production, Ernest Bevin as Minister of Labour and National Service and Sir Kingsley Wood, now Chancellor of the Exchequer. Sir John Anderson replaced Chamberlain as Lord President in October and Anthony Eden took over as Foreign Secretary in December. Various changes were made subsequently but the membership never exceeded eight until the end of the coalition in May 1945.

Some ministers and officials who were not in the War Cabinet were regularly present at its meetings and were known as 'constant attenders'. They included the service ministers and Chiefs of Staff, while other ministers were liable to be summoned for items of business in which they had a special interest. Matters brought before the War Cabinet embraced major foreign policy issues, questions of a predominantly political character or any problem, whether civil or military, on which a decision could only be given at the highest level. Bridges, as Secretary, was present at practically all meetings; Ismay, in his capacity as Deputy Secretary (Military), attended all at which military matters were being discussed; and one or more Assistant Secretaries, both civil and military, were also generally present. The War Cabinet, as under Lloyd George, was supported by layers of standing and *ad hoc* committees and the efficiency of this machinery was enhanced by the existence of the single War Cabinet Secretariat, whose members constituted an invaluable liaison network. It was the daily and even hourly contact between the members of the Secretariat which enabled any subject to be steered towards the most appropriate body and helped to avoid conflicts of jurisdiction.

The most far-reaching modification which Churchill made to this machinery was to combine the office of Prime Minister with that of Minister of Defence. The powers of the new office were left undefined and Churchill saw no need to create a 'ministry' in the accepted sense, his staff being provided by the military branch of the War Cabinet Secretariat, headed by Ismay, Hollis and Jacob. Ismay, now a Major-General, was appointed as Chief of Staff to the Minister of Defence and joined the Chiefs of Staff Committee, with Hollis taking his place as Secretary to that body. What this change achieved was to enable Churchill to exercise a direct personal supervision, not only over the formulation of military policy and planning but also over the day-to-day conduct of operations through the Chiefs of Staff. Decisions could now be reached and translated into action much more quickly than under the previous system. The service ministers, from May 1940 on, were primarily occupied with matters of organisation and administration.

The Military Co-ordination Committee was supplanted by the Defence Committee, over which Churchill presided. This was divided into two panels, the Defence Committee (Operations) and the Defence Committee (Supply). The Defence Committee (Operations) was, for a while, Churchill's principal instrument for conducting the war, and was originally composed of the service ministers and Chiefs of Staff. Attlee, Beaverbrook and Eden were soon added and other ministers attended when required. According to Ismay, its great virtue was that, for the first time, 'the Chiefs of Staff were in direct and continuous contact with the Head of the Government, and were able to act as a combined Battle Headquarters'. Indeed, the Defence Committee declined in importance after 1941 as Churchill worked more and more through 'Staff Conferences' – meetings of the Chiefs of Staff Committee at which the Prime Minister took the chair.

The Chiefs of Staff also met alone, with one of their own number in the chair and with Vice-Admiral Lord Louis Mountbatten, as Chief of Combined Operations, joining them whenever questions

FACING PAGE TOP Winston Churchill broadcasting from No. 10, Downing Street during the Second World War. He is wearing his famous wartime 'siren suit'. *IWM H 20446*

FACING PAGE BELOW Churchill's War Cabinet, photographed in the garden of No. 10 Downing Street in 1941. In the back row, from left to right are: Arthur Greenwood, Ernest Bevin, Lord Beaverbrook and Sir Kingsley Wood. Seated in front, from left to right, are: Sir John Anderson, Winston Churchill, Clement Attlee and Anthony Eden. *(Central Press)*

ABOVE Members of the Defence Committee in the garden of No. 10 Downing Street in 1941. Seen in the back row, from left to right, are: Air Chief Marshal Sir Charles Portal, Chief of the Air Staff; Admiral of the Fleet Sir Dudley Pound, First Sea Lord and Chief of the Naval Staff; Sir Archibald Sinclair, Secretary of State for Air; David Margesson, Secretary of State for War; General Sir John Dill, Chief of the Imperial General Staff; Major-General Sir Hastings Ismay, Chief of Staff to the Minister of Defence and Deputy Secretary (Military) to the War Cabinet; Colonel Leslie Hollis, Senior Assistant Secretary (Military) to the War Cabinet and Secretary to the Chiefs of Staff Committee. Those in the front row, from left to right, are: Lord Beaverbrook, Minister of Aircraft Production; Clement Attlee, Lord Privy Seal; Winston Churchill, Prime Minister and Minister of Defence; Anthony Eden, Foreign Secretary; and A V Alexander, First Lord of the Admiralty. *IWM HU 3207* of overall strategy or combined operations were discussed. As a vital element in Churchill's system of direction they had a vast range of responsibilities and had to focus their attention alike on immediate operational problems and wider issues of future policy. The Deputy Chiefs of Staff ceased to function but from April 1940 there was a Vice-Chiefs of Staff Committee to share part of the burden, and the subordinate bodies for planning and intelligence were reorganised and expanded. In September 1940 the Joint Planning Staff, as it was now called, was split into three sections for Strategical, Executive and Future Operational Planning. Liaison officers from civil departments were attached to each section. The Joint Intelligence Committee was enlarged to incorporate a Joint Intelligence Staff, drawn from representatives of the three services, the Foreign Office and the Ministry of Economic Warfare, as well as an Intelligence Section (Operations) which supplied information to commanders and planners about areas likely to become the scene of operations.

In civil matters, the counterpart of the Defence Committee was the Lord President's Committee, chaired by Anderson from October 1940 to September 1943 and thereafter by Attlee. Its main function was to co-ordinate the work of the Production Council and the Economic Policy, Food Policy, Home Policy and Civil Defence Committees. The success achieved by Anderson and Attlee in managing this body gave Churchill more freedom to concentrate on the military aspects of the war, and the Lord President's Committee not merely survived until the end of the war but extended its powers to become the supreme organ, under the War Cabinet, for the control of all matters affecting the home front.

THE CABINET WAR ROOM IN THE SUMMER OF 1940 ■■■

C hurchill's accession to power, coinciding as it did with the intensification of the war in Europe, signalled the start of a new phase of activity in the basement beneath the New Public Offices. The most pressing problems were caused by the arrival in the summer of 1940 of elements of the Home Defence Executive, which had been hastily created in May when the collapse of France began to appear inevitable. It consisted of the Commander-in-Chief, Home Forces, and representatives of the Admiralty, Air Ministry, Ministry of Home Security and the main Royal Air Force Commands, under the chairmanship of the Chief Civil Staff Officer to the C-in-C, Home Forces, Sir Findlater Stewart. At this time the GHQ, Home Forces, was located at Kneller Hall in Twickenham, but on 29 May the War Cabinet approved a recommendation from the Chiefs of Staff that an Advanced Headquarters should be set up in the Cabinet War Room, as the place best served by communications and where the C-in-C, Home Forces, General Sir Edmund Ironside, would have instant access to the Prime Minister. It was from this Advanced Headquarters that the defence of Britain would be conducted in the event of invasion.

Faced with this sudden demand for extra accommodation, Hollis planned to give Room 64, which was now being used as a Map Room Annexe, to the Advanced Headquarters of the GHQ, Home Forces, as its operational map room. However, it proved too small, so the main Map Room had to absorb the additional component, with Room 64 serving as overflow accommodation and as an area for the preparation of intelligence summaries. By July, when the main body of GHQ, Home Forces, moved to St Paul's School in Hammersmith, the Advanced Headquarters had been allotted several rooms in the War Room complex. Room 62B, near the Map Room, was allocated to the C-in-C, Home Forces; six of his senior staff officers were to work in Room 62A and five junior staff officers would be in Room 62. Room 69A, next to the Cabinet Room, was partitioned for use by Sir Findlater Stewart and two of his assistants. A signals office was set up in the sub-basement and clerks and typists of the Intelligence and Operations sections also moved into the Dock. On 29 July the Advanced Headquarters was sufficiently well-established to hold a full-scale manning exercise in the War Room. General Sir Alan Brooke, who had succeeded Ironside nine days earlier, subsequently made the wry comment that the only fault of the Advanced Headquarters was 'its proximity to Winston'.

The arrival of the Advanced Headquarters exacerbated the problem of housing the Joint Planners, whose expansion was already regarded as the main cause of overcrowding in the basement. Rooms 62, 62A and 62B had been among the areas temporarily occupied by them, but suggestions that the Joint Planners should move out to Richmond Terrace or be shifted into the Dock were rejected by Ismay, who insisted, early in June, that the War Room itself must expand to house the Joint Planners at basement level, thus keeping the Dock as a reserve of accommodation for future emergencies. The Office of Works yet again had to yield space and cleared Rooms 57A, 58 and 59, at the southern end of the basement corridor, for the Joint Planning Staff.

Unlike Chamberlain, who rarely visited the War Room, Churchill quickly made his presence felt there. Hollis has related how one evening in May 1940, shortly after becoming Prime Minister, Churchill entered the underground Cabinet Room and declared: 'This is the room from which I'll direct the war'. Even if his sweeping prediction was not entirely fulfilled in the coming years, Churchill

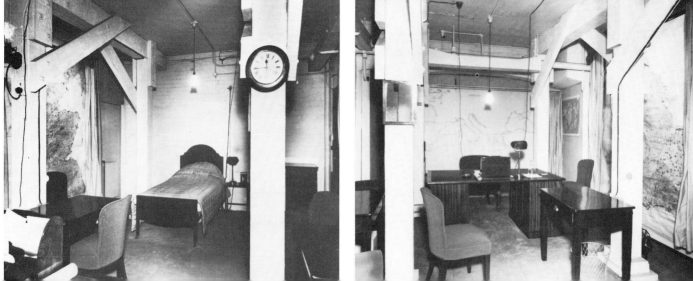

nonetheless made extensive use of the basement's facilities. On 27 July he was given Room 65A, the former Cabinet Room, for his personal use as a combined office and bedroom and this remained as his emergency accommodation in the basement until the end of the war. His immediate staff, including Ismay and three Private Secretaries, were allocated Rooms 66, 66A and 66B, adjacent to Churchill's room and reached by means of a narrow sub-corridor leading off the northern half of the main corridor. These three offices had previously formed part of the Office of Works strong room area. The remaining room in this area, Room 67, was designated as a conference room for the Chiefs of Staff, since Room 64 had now become the Map Room Annexe. Churchill's War Cabinet met in the basement for the first time on 29 July but held no further meetings in Room 69 until the commencement of the Blitz in September.

THE BLITZ AND THE CONSTRUCTION OF THE SLAB

As the pressure on accommodation in the basement grew during the summer of 1940, the Office of Works made a sustained effort to persuade the central organs of government and command to leave the War Room, arguing that the existing scale of protection was inadequate and that a bomb falling into one of the inner courtyards of the New Public Offices might penetrate into the Dock and shock the whole building. On 8 June, de Normann wrote to Ismay that the War Room could not be made safe against a direct hit with a heavy bomb, and suggested the War Cabinet should go to 'Paddock' at Dollis Hill, which was now complete and believed to be proof against 500 lb bombs. The force of these arguments was considerably strengthened when the German air attacks on London began in earnest on 7 September. Until then, Churchill had been under the impression that the War Room was bomb-proof and was startled to discover that this was not the case.

The persistent air raids in late September and early October hardened Churchill's resolve to improve the quality of protection available for the War Cabinet and essential staffs. At the end of September a bomb narrowly missed the New Public Offices, making a crater near the Clive Steps at the north-western corner of the building. Then, on the evening of 14 October, bombs struck the Treasury and Horse Guards Parade, causing blast damage to the kitchen, pantry and offices on the Treasury side of No. 10 Downing Street. Churchill was already convinced that he and his personal staff should move out of Downing Street and in the last fortnight of September preparations had been put in hand for them to transfer to a suite of rooms on the ground and first floors of the New Public Offices, overlooking St James's Park. The raids also induced the War Cabinet to make greater use of the emergency accommodation in the War Room.

The majority of meetings of the War Cabinet in September, October and November 1940 were held in the underground Cabinet Room (Room 69), and almost all of the meetings of the Defence Committee (Operations) took place there that autumn and winter. In this room, baize-covered tables were arranged in a hollow square to seat 25 people. Churchill sat in a large wooden chair on the western side of the room, in front of a map of the world. Behind his chair was a fire bucket, strategically placed to serve as a receptacle for his cigar ends. Other ministers and officials sat on tubular metal chairs with green upholstery. At meetings of the War Cabinet, Chamberlain, and later Attlee, sat on Churchill's immediate left, with Bridges and Ismay to the Prime Minister's right. When the Defence Committee met, the Chiefs of Staff sat at the top table, but on the inside of the hollow square facing Churchill. Outside the room, a small lobby was built and fitted with an outer and inner door, which were both locked during meetings. A sentry patrolled in the main corridor and another stood on duty between the two doors. A small glass aperture, reinforced by mesh, in the inner door enabled the second sentry to watch, though not to hear, the ministers inside. Within the room, just above the inner door, were red and green bulbs which showed whether or not an air raid was in progress.

One War Cabinet meeting was held at 'Paddock' on 3 October, but the ministers disliked it and the Dollis Hill citadel was visited only once more, in March 1941. Churchill was determined that the Government should 'not be beaten out of London' and regarded 'Paddock' as a place of last resort, telling Bridges that the War Cabinet 'cannot live and work there for weeks on end, while leaving the great part of their staffs less well provided for than they are now in Whitehall'. On 22 October 1940 the Prime Minister authorised the provision of a 'substantial measure of overhead cover above the War Room' and also entrusted Lord Beaverbrook with the task of supervising the conversion of a number of the more modern buildings in and around Whitehall into alternative bombproof citadels. Top priority was given to the completion of a Whitehall Deep Tunnel, which was intended to offer secure communications and access between these various strongholds, and certain buildings were selected for strengthening, including the Faraday Building in Queen Victoria Street and a steel-framed building in Horseferry Road.

So far as the Cabinet War Room was concerned, the immediate outcome of Churchill's decision of 22 October was that, in the fol-

42

TOP Churchill inspecting the bomb crater at the north-western corner of the New Public Offices on 30 September 1940. Sir John Anderson is standing on the far right of the photograph. The present public entrance to the Cabinet War Rooms is very close to the spot where this bomb fell. *IWM F 1338*

BOTTOM The interior of a Secretary's office in No. 10 Downing Street, showing the blast damage caused by a bomb which fell on the Treasury on the evening of 14 October 1940. *IWM F 1725*

RIGHT A Heinkel He 111 bomber over London on 7 September 1940. *IWM C 5422*

lowing weeks, the sub-ground floor above the basement along the western side of the New Public Offices was filled in with a reinforced concrete slab. Rolled steel joists, supported by brick piers in the basement corridor, were installed above the existing ceiling of the basement, and on top of these were placed steel trough sections which formed the base for the concrete slab. The slab itself, which was three feet thick, was reinforced with layers of steel rails and tramlines. A concrete apron wall, built along the external wall of the New Public Offices at ground level, was expected to prevent bombs from causing damage to the basement at the point where the slab ended. The space below the staircase leading to the War Room from the entrance on the St James's Park side also had to be filled with concrete to plug a dangerous gap in the defences. The Camp Commandant's office (Room 63), which occupied this space, was therefore lost together with the corresponding area in the Dock below. In the War Room corridor traverses were constructed at intervals to diffuse the effects of shock waves. Churchill took a close interest in this work, often clambering over girders and temporary walls to proffer advice to the workmen about bricklaying or the construction of a traverse. On one such occasion the Prime Minister leapt off a girder into a pool of liquid cement and his feet became embedded.

From the middle of October, while the suite above ground in the New Public Offices was being prepared, Churchill spent most nights in a shelter constructed for the Railway Executive Committee in a disused tube station at Down Street, near Piccadilly. He seldom slept in his basement bedroom beneath the New Public Offices during the Blitz and only used it for this purpose on 16 and 18 September and again on 28 October. However, he did make a number of broadcasts from this room, including an invasion warning on 11 September, a broadcast to the French people in both English and French on 21 October, and one to the Italian people on 23 December. He also broadcast from the room on 8 December 1941, following the outbreak of war with Japan. The Prime Minister and Mrs Churchill finally moved into their new quarters in December 1940 and lived there for the rest of the war, the suite becoming known as the 'No. 10 Downing Street Annexe'. Here, to the right of the entrance on the ground floor of the building, as one approached it from St James's Park, the Prime Minister and Mrs Churchill had their private apartments, including bedrooms, a dining room and a sitting room, the windows of which were protected by steel shutters. The Prime Minister's Private Secretaries had rooms nearby and there was also a private map room for the Prime Minister on this floor, run by Captain Richard Pim, RNVR. On the first floor were the offices of Churchill's personal assistant, Major Desmond Morton, his ADC, Commander C R Thompson RN, and his scientific adviser, Professor Frederick Lindemann. Bridges,

Ismay, Hollis, Jacob and other members of the War Cabinet Secretariat were given rooms on the second floor, along the Great George Street side.

The structural protection of the building was supplemented by local defence schemes in the critical months of 1940. In May a sandbag pillbox was erected at the corner of Great George Street and Horse Guards Road from which members of the Home Guard could cover the access routes with machine guns. Later the Royal Marine orderlies who performed the basic security duties in the War Room were augmented by a small detachment of Grenadier Guards, known collectively as 'Rance's Guard'. The latter were stationed permanently at the ground floor entrance to the Cabinet War Room, which was located at the top of a short flight of steps leading from the main door on the St James's Park side and which adjoined the entrance to the 'No. 10 Annexe'. A machine gun post was sited here to cover the entrances. In the basement itself the defence would be conducted by the Royal Marines, under the command of the Camp Commandant or the Map Room Duty Officer. The Map Room staff and the Joint Planners would arm themselves and act as a reserve if needed. Rifle racks were fitted to the walls of the basement for just such a contingency.

One of George Rance's many jobs as civilian custodian of the War Room was to adjust the indicator boards in a wooden holder attached to the wall of the basement corridor. These boards gave news of the weather outside to those working underground. During heavy raids Rance, as a private joke, would put up the board marked 'Windy'. Not surprisingly, the continuous raids, coupled with the loss of the sub-ground floor dormitories to the slab, led to an increased use of the emergency sleeping accommodation in the Dock. Many still preferred to go home to their London flats or to their clubs even during the worst bombing, since the presence of rats, the ever-burning electric lights and the constant hum of ventilation machinery were not conducive to sleep in the sub-basement. All the same, the Dock was often utilised by Map Room officers on night watches and by those secretaries and typists who worked late after evening meetings of the War Cabinet and Defence Committee so that the minutes would be produced ready for circulation the next morning. The slab gave an added feeling of security to staff using the sub-basement and they were therefore able to work in the War Room and 'No. 10 Annexe' above without undue tension.

LEFT This photograph, taken in 1945, shows the main doorway to the 'No. 10 Annexe' on the ground floor of the New Public Offices, with a Royal Marine orderly standing just inside. The armed sentry on duty outside is standing on coconut and rubber mats, which were intended to deaden the sound of his feet when he came to attention. The partly-open steel door in the blast wall on the left of the picture was the main wartime entrance to the Cabinet War Room, which was reached by a flight of stone steps leading down to the basement. *IWM MH 520*

RIGHT A Royal Marine orderly on duty behind the blast wall at the ground-floor entrance to the Cabinet War Room. Note the machine-gun slit and the bells used to summon the emergency guards. *(Paul Popper)*

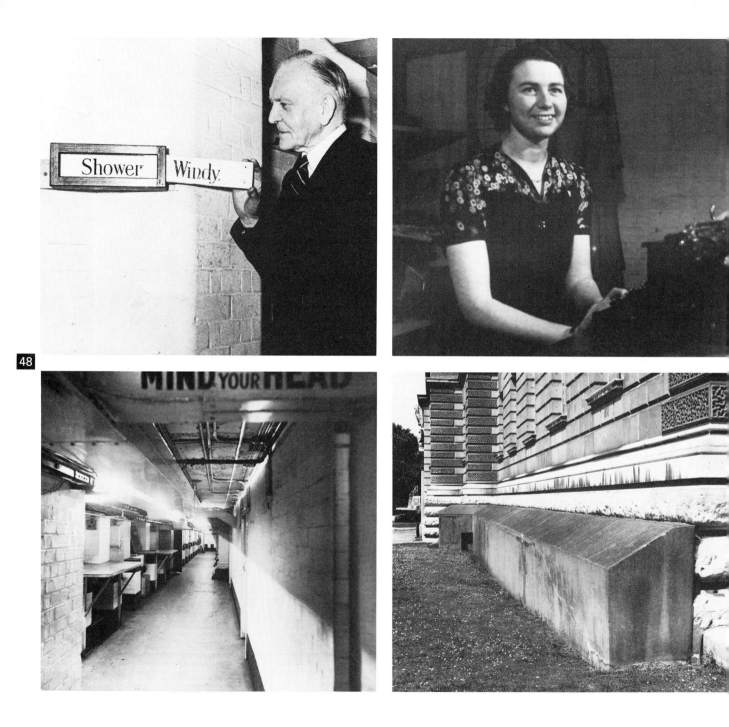

ABOVE LEFT George Rance adjusting the weather indicator boards in the main corridor of the Cabinet War Room. When a heavy raid was in progress above, Rance, as a private joke, would put up the board bearing the word 'Windy'. *IWM HU 43777*

ABOVE RIGHT Miss Margaret Lindars at her desk in the Joint Planning Staff typing pool in Room 60A. This is one of the few photographs known to have been taken in the Cabinet War Room in the early part of the Second World War. *Courtesy of Mr and Mrs R Smith*

BELOW LEFT The main corridor of the sub-basement or 'Dock', looking south. The emergency sleeping quarters for the Map Room officers were on the right of the corridor as one looks at the photograph. *IWM MH 533*

BELOW RIGHT The concrete apron wall erected along the western side of the building in 1940 to prevent possible blast damage to the Cabinet War Room at the point where its overhead protection ended. Much of this apron wall can still be seen today. *IWM 82/20/180*

THE COURTYARD ROOMS AND THE CABINET WAR ROOM ANNEXE

Almost from the outset the Prime Minister was eager for the slab to be extended towards the centre of the New Public Offices and by late December 1940 it not only covered Courts 11, 12 and 13, just beyond the existing War Room, but also the larger West Court, which was even nearer the centre of the block. The extension of the slab in this direction was encouraged by General Brooke, who wished to move the operational staff of the GHQ, Home Forces, into the New Public Offices to be closer to the War Office and other departments in Whitehall. The staff of GHQ, Home Forces, now numbered around 500 officers and other ranks, and a considerable proportion of these were installed in some forty rooms in the basement under the West Court by the beginning of 1941. This area was subsequently referred to as the 'CWR Annexe'. The Advanced Headquarters moved out of the original War Room basement to join the main body on 12 January 1941.

In the spring of 1941 the rooms under Courts 11, 12 and 13, between the original War Room and the 'CWR Annexe', gradually became available. The installation of the concrete slab here added a further thirty-four rooms to the overall complex. The southernmost rooms of this group, under Court 13, were used to house a main telephone exchange, a first-aid room and a canteen. The rooms off the middle section of the courtyard corridor, under Court 12, were given over to the Prime Minister, his personal staff and War Cabinet ministers. Anderson, Attlee, Beaverbrook and Eden all had rooms in this part of the basement. The Prime Minister's rooms included a bedroom for Mrs Churchill and a small dining room, with a kitchen to serve it. The Chiefs of Staff were allocated a reserve conference room next to the kitchen. The rooms to the north, under Court 11, were largely for members of the War Cabinet Secretariat. Ironically, the Blitz had passed its peak by the time these rooms were ready for occupation and they were kept mainly as a refuge to be used if there was a resumption of heavy bombing. Ministers occasionally used their rooms after working late, and the Prime Minister's daughter, Miss Mary Churchill (now Lady Soames), sometimes slept in Mrs Churchill's room when on leave from the ATS, but most preferred to carry on their work above ground. The Chiefs of Staff now often met on the second floor of the building, while 'Staff Conferences' were frequently held in the Prime Minister's ground floor map room.

Up to February 1941, only 146 high-explosive bombs had fallen within 1,000 yards of the Cenotaph and no disastrous damage had yet been caused to the surrounding Government buildings, facts which appeared to justify Churchill's decision to keep the central organs of government in Whitehall. However, it was still essential for the New Public Offices to have a high degree of protection. On 13 February 1941 Churchill inspected the slab and gave orders for it to be extended again, this time in the direction of the Great George Street side of the building, towards the south side of Court 14. By April the Air Ministry had asked for similar cover for the King Charles Street side, where their own War Room was located. This resulted in the provision of new protected areas under Courts 7 and 8. The concrete cover crept on inexorably until November 1941, prompting Lawrence Burgis to dub it the 'Never-Ending Slab'.

The expansion of the War Room complex did not wholly solve the overcrowding problem, although from mid-1941 some relief was afforded by the progress being achieved at the Horseferry Road citadel, which was ready for at least partial occupation by August of that year. In September it was agreed that elements of the Air Ministry staff would move to Horseferry Road at the end of the year. The following April, the Chiefs of Staff and Sir John Anderson proposed that the GHQ, Home Forces, should also go to Horseferry Road. The construction of the extension of the Whitehall Deep Tunnel to this citadel was completed in August 1942 and GHQ, Home Forces, had actually moved there by November. Soon afterwards the Joint Planning Staff and the Joint Intelligence Committee, which had previously been spread all over the New Public Offices, occupied the rooms in the 'CWR Annexe' thus vacated by GHQ, Home Forces, and stayed in the area under the West Court until the end of the war. The Joint Planners now included the so-called London Controlling Section, a cover name given to a group responsible for deception plans intended to divert enemy resources away from genuine Allied operations. The concentration of most of the planning and intelligence bodies in one area greatly facilitated Allied preparations for the forthcoming landings in occupied Europe.

LIFE IN THE CABINET WAR ROOM, 1941–1944

After December 1940, the War Cabinet as a body used the original nucleus of rooms in the western basement much less frequently and, once the really heavy raids on London ceased in May 1941, meetings were normally held at 10 Downing Street – the traditional venue – or at the House of Commons. The War Cabinet met in the War Room five times in 1942 and only twice in 1943. Sir Rupert Howorth retired as Deputy Secretary (Civil) to the War Cabinet in March 1942 and was succeeded by Norman Brook. When Brook was appointed Permanent Secretary to the Ministry of Reconstruction in December 1943, he was replaced by two

Under-Secretaries (Civil), Sir Gilbert Laithwaite and W S Murrie. In 1942 Captain C F Battiscombe became Camp Commandant of the War Room, but Lawrence Burgis took on these duties when ill-health caused Battiscombe to retire the following year.

The increasing tendency of the Chiefs of Staff and other bodies to meet upstairs in the building, and the moves, first of the GHQ, Home Forces, and later of the Joint Planners, to the 'CWR Annexe', permitted some re-allocation of rooms in the western basement. Hollis took over Sir Findlater Stewart's former room, 69A, as his own emergency accommodation, and Room 67, no longer needed by the Chiefs of Staff, was reserved for the Prime Minister's Private Office staff, with the adjacent Room 66B being allocated to John Martin, Churchill's Principal Private Secretary. Room 62B became the Camp Commandant's office after the loss of the original Room 63 to the slab. The Royal Marine detachment, having already expanded from ten to forty-nine by August 1942, was increased by a further fifteen, at Ismay's request, that November and Room 62A was turned into a Royal Marines Mess. Next door, Room 62 was made an emergency office for the personal secretaries and typists of the War Cabinet Secretariat.

To the south of these rooms, Bridges retained the right-hand, or northern half of Room 61A, with his Private Secretaries in the left-hand portion. Ismay, having been allocated space at the northern end of the corridor in 1940, reverted to using the right-hand half of Room 61 as his emergency quarters by mid-1941. In the other half was his Private Secretary, initially Paymaster Commander M H Knott RN and later Paymaster Lieutenant-Commander I P McEwan RNVR. The Joint Planning Staff typists left Room 60A in the summer of 1941, ultimately going to the 'CWR Annexe', and enabling Room 60A to be partitioned for use by Lawrence Burgis and by John Winnifrith, the Establishment Officer of the War Cabinet Office. In the latter part of the war the two halves of this room were reserved for Sir Gilbert Laithwaite and Colonel D C Capel-Dunn, Secretary of the Joint Intelligence Committee. The War Cabinet Office switchboard was shifted temporarily to the Courtyard Rooms in 1941 and the northern half of Room 60 subsequently became an office for the Royal Marines. The BBC equipment was still kept in the left-hand part of Room 60, but since it was not used often enough to warrant a room to itself, a combined War Cabinet Office and No. 10 Downing Street switchboard was eventually placed here. Because they were intended mainly as emergency accommodation, few of these southern rooms were in continuous occupation.

By contrast, the Map Room remained the heart of the Cabinet War Room and was manned day and night throughout the war. In the southern half of the room were the long tables at which the Map

ABOVE TOP Room 69A, at the extreme north-eastern end of the original Cabinet War Room corridor. This room was allocated first to Sir Findlater Stewart and then to Leslie Hollis, whose cap can just be seen towards the left of the photograph. Hollis was promoted to the rank of Major-General in 1943. *(Paul Popper)*

ABOVE BELOW General Ismay's room (Room 61 Right) off the southern part of the basement corridor. *(Paul Popper)*

RIGHT Switchboard operators at work in Room 60 Left in 1945. The combined War Cabinet Office and No. 10 Downing Street switchboard seen here had three times the capacity of the smaller switchboard which had been located in the room next door earlier in the war. The top of the steel cabinet containing the BBC outside broadcast equipment can be seen beyond the switchboard, to the right of the door. *(Paul Popper)*

Room officers sat, with the Duty Officer, who was drawn from each of the three services in rotation, occupying a place at the northern end of these tables. Down the centre of the tables ran a wooden bridge on which stood the coloured telephones, linked to the service War Rooms and other key points and known to the Map Room officers as the 'beauty chorus'. The telephones had flashing lights as an alternative to bells and three were also fitted with scramblers, a device that rendered the conversation meaningless and just a jumble of noise until it was unscrambled at the receiving end. The boxes containing the scrambler equipment were situated in a wooden trough below the telephone bridge.

Virtually the whole of the southern wall of the room was covered by a large map of the world, on which the position of convoys and the movements of individual warships were plotted. During the war this map became so perforated with pin-holes that the outlines of the principal convoy routes could be seen from the other end of the room. At the northern end was a large map of the Pacific theatre and next to it, in the north-eastern corner near the Map Room door, was another showing the positions of the German and Russian armies on the Eastern Front. The latter map can be seen today in the Map Room Annexe. The routine tasks of the Map Room officers included the preparation of a weekly resumé of events for the Chiefs of Staff and the production of a daily news-sheet, the 'Cabinet War Room Record', some fifteen copies of which were duplicated for the War Cabinet and others, with one copy being taken to Buckingham Palace by the Duty Officer every morning.

The Mess in Room 68 inevitably became a focal point of life in the Cabinet War Room, offering precious moments of relaxation to staff who, under Churchill's dynamic but demanding leadership, worked extremely long hours at considerable pressure. Behind a curtain in one corner of Room 68 were a sink and a small electric cooker where Royal Marine orderlies prepared simple snacks, such as Welsh rarebit, soup and bacon and eggs. Cold ham, tongue and biscuits and cheese were also staple fare. In the opposite corner was the steel cabinet containing drinks. It was only during the last six months of the war that a ration of two large whiskies and two large gins per person per day was introduced.

Off the eastern side of the basement corridor, near the Map Room, was a small cell-like room once used by George Rance for the storage of cleaning materials and as a place for issuing the pay of Office of Works cleaning staff. After America's entry into the war in December 1941, this tiny room assumed an importance out of all proportion to its size for it was from here that Churchill had a direct telephone link to President Roosevelt in the White House. The outer door was fitted with a lock taken from a toilet and marked 'Vacant' and 'Engaged'. Inside, on a baize-covered table, stood the specially

RIGHT The main corridor of the Cabinet War Room, looking north. The door to the Map Room (Room 65) is on the left of the photograph. The figure on the right is Colour-Sergeant Frederick Hunt, a member of the Royal Marine detachment which was permanently on duty in the basement. *IWM MH 534*

RIGHT Map Room officers on duty in the main Map Room in May 1945. Those who can be identified are: Commander R Bosanquet RN (standing, third from right); Wing Commander J S Heagerty RAF (seated, second from right); and Wing Commander E T Rees RAF (seated, far right). Heagerty, as Duty Officer for this particular watch, is sitting at the northern end of the tables. The large map of the Pacific theatre is visible at the far end of the room. *IWM MH 27688*

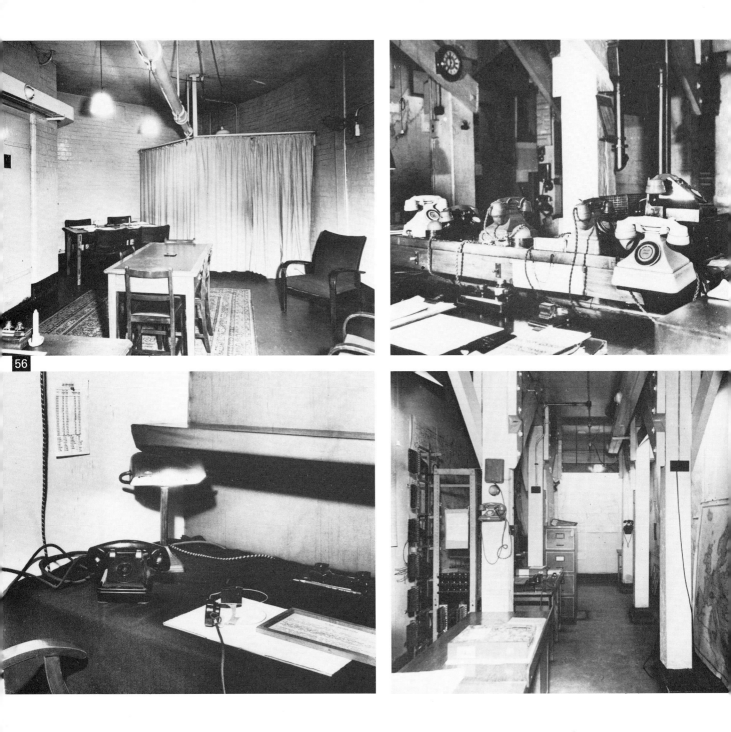

56

LEFT The Mess Room (Room 68) at the northern end of the basement corridor. The curtain in the corner of the room hides the sink and the small electric cooker where Royal Marine orderlies prepared simple meals for those working in the Cabinet War Room. *IWM MH 532*

RIGHT The 'beauty chorus' of telephones in the Map Room. The white telephone in the right foreground was a direct line to the Secretary's Office in No. 10 Downing Street, while those to its left were direct lines to the individual service War Rooms. The indicator lights which were fitted as an alternative to bells may be seen next to the telephones on the narrow wooden bridge between the tables. *(Paul Popper)*

RIGHT This close-up of the Convoy Map on the southern wall of the Map Room clearly illustrates the mass of pinholes caused by the constant plotting of convoy and warship movements during the Second World War. *IWM HU 43544*

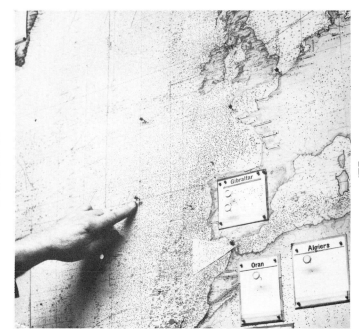

LEFT The interior of the small transatlantic telephone room in the Cabinet War Room basement, showing the special telephone used by Winston Churchill to talk to President Roosevelt in the White House. The 'X-Ray Instructions', seen at the bottom right of the picture, warned the user to speak directly into the instrument in a normal voice, since loud speech was likely to impair the quality of transmission. On the wall to the left is the chart stating the difference in times between Britain and America. *(Paul Popper)*

RIGHT The Map Room Annexe (Room 64), which was used as overflow accommodation for the main Map Room and as a place for the writing of reports and intelligence summaries. The telephone switch frame on the left enabled individual officers and officials to make secure calls from their own rooms using a single scrambler on a time-sharing basis. *IWM MH 528* adapted American telephone, and on the wall to the right was a clock with two black hands showing London time and two red hands giving the corresponding time in Washington. To the left hung a chart stating the difference in times between Britain and America.

Throughout the Second World War, all transatlantic calls were sent by radio-telephony. Security for this limited system was initially provided by advanced commercial scramblers such as the Bell Telephone A3. The link was not, in fact, immune from enemy interception and great caution had to be exercised by anyone using the system. In October 1940, the Bell Telephone Laboratories in the United States began work on 'Project X', the development of a machine capable of producing secure speech transmission by radio-telephony. By early 1943, three production machines had been built and it was proposed to install them in Washington, London and Algiers. The machines were officially named 'SIGSALY' by the United States Army Signal Corps. The London machine was code-named 'X-Ray' and was shipped from America on the RMS *Queen Elizabeth* in May 1943. Due to its immense size, it proved impossible to fit the whole device into the Cabinet War Room and the main body of the machine was installed in the basement of Selfridge's department store in Oxford Street. The Prime Minister's private terminal in the War Room was equipped with an intermediate scrambler linked to Selfridge's by an underground cable. 'X-Ray' became operational in August 1943 although the evidence suggests that Churchill did not use the system until April 1944. A card containing instructions for the use of 'X-Ray' was placed near the special telephone in the War Room basement.

FROM THE V-WEAPONS OFFENSIVE TO VICTORY AND BEYOND

Late in 1942 and early in 1943, doubts were voiced about the degree of cover provided by the slab, particularly in the courtyard areas which were not protected by the upper floors of the New Public Offices. A report submitted in March 1943 by the Research and Experimental Section of the Ministry of Home Security implied that anything heavier than a 500 lb bomb might cause serious damage, but the chances of a single raid inflicting casualties on those under the slab were put at less than one in eight hundred. It was then felt that the current deployment and state of the Luftwaffe precluded a recurrence of the Blitz and the War Cabinet Secretariat took the view that any extra work on the New Public Offices would not confer sufficient additional protection to warrant the cost and inconvenience involved. Even so, the doubts were strong

RIGHT Winston Churchill leaving the New Public Offices by the St. James's Park entrance early in 1944. Note the barbed-wire defences in the background. *(Keystone)*

LEFT A meeting of the Chiefs of Staff Committee in progress on the second floor of the New Public Offices in 1945. Those present, reading from left to right, are: Major-General Hollis (Secretary); Admiral of the Fleet Sir Andrew Cunningham; Field-Marshal Sir Alan Brooke (Chairman); Marshal of the Royal Air Force Sir Charles Portal; General Sir Hastings Ismay; Colonel C R Price (Assistant Secretary). *IWM HU 43346* enough for the War Cabinet Secretariat to begin looking for alternative accommodation for the War Cabinet and Chiefs of Staff when, in the spring of 1943, the Government received advanced warning of the likelihood of attack by flying bombs and rockets. In July and August 1943 plans were made to prepare the basement of the North Rotunda at Horseferry Road for possible use by the Prime Minister, his personal staff and a nucleus of the War Cabinet Secretariat. These quarters, code-named 'Anson', were ready on 15 November but in February 1944 Churchill repeated that he had no intention of moving unless London suffered a scale of attack far worse than anything experienced to date.

The attack on London by V-1 flying bombs started on 13 June 1944 and six days later, on 19 June, the War Cabinet met in the War Room for the first time that year. It held all its meetings there until 9 September, a time when the British defences had begun to master the flying bombs and the V-2 rocket attack had not yet approached its peak. The numbers of rockets launched against London steadily increased in the following months and on 9 January 1945 the War Cabinet returned to the War Room. All but a few of its meetings took place in the basement between then and 28 March, the day on which the last flying bombs reached London. After that date, ministers generally met at 10 Downing Street and did not go back to the War Room. In all, 115 out of the 1,188 meetings of the War Cabinet from September 1939 to July 1945 were held in the basement beneath the New Public Offices.

When the war in Europe ended with Germany's surrender in May 1945, the underground protection for the War Cabinet was no longer needed and the rooms above and below ground in the New Public Offices were gradually vacated and turned over to more peaceful uses, though the Map Room was kept operational until a cease-fire was imposed in South-East Asia and the Pacific on 15 August. After the formal surrender of Japan in September 1945, the majority of the rooms in the basement were stripped of their wartime furniture and equipment. Part of the basement became a teleprinter centre and later a television conference centre for the Chiefs of Staff and, for a time, Rooms 62, 62A and 62B were used respectively as a conference room, a teleprinter room and a cypher room. However, a number of the original rooms, including the Map Room and its Annexe, the Cabinet Room, Churchill's combined office and bedroom and the transatlantic telephone room were left just as they had been in the last days of the war. In 1948 these important rooms were made into a museum following an announcement in Parliament by the then Minister of Works that they would be preserved for posterity.

The rooms remained under the care of the Cabinet Office and were opened to the public on a limited footing, visitors being permitted to view them only by special arrangement. During these years the term 'Cabinet War Rooms', in the plural, came into increasing use, as it gave a more accurate impression of the nature of the underground complex than was conveyed by the wartime title. Responsibility for the Cabinet War Rooms was transferred to the Department of the Environment in 1975, but access to them was still restricted to those who made a prior appointment. In 1981 the Prime Minister, Mrs Margaret Thatcher, decided that this historic site should become more freely accessible to visitors by being opened on a regular basis. The Property Services Agency of the Department of the Environment then invited the Imperial War Museum to administer the Cabinet War Rooms on its behalf and, following a period of necessary restoration and conservation work, they were duly reopened to the public in 1984. Many of the rooms emptied in 1945, particularly at the southern end of the basement corridor, have been painstakingly recreated in their original wartime appearance. The Cabinet War Rooms are now preserved as a permanent reminder of the way in which Britain's war effort was directed in the momentous years from 1939 to 1945.

RIGHT External view of the western side of the New Public Offices in 1945. The barbed-wire defences have been dismantled, but the protective steel shutters are still in place at the ground floor windows. *IWM HU 43773*

THE WAR CABINET
3 SEPTEMBER 1939–
10 MAY 1940

(Where no terminal date is given the minister in question remained a member of the War Cabinet until the end of the period)

Name	Office held in War Cabinet	Dates of membership
Rt Hon Neville Chamberlain MP	Prime Minister and First Lord of the Treasury	3 September 1939
Rt Hon Lord Chatfield GCB OM KCMG CVO	Minister for the Co-ordination of Defence	3 September 1939– 3 April 1940
Rt Hon Winston S Churchill MP	First Lord of the Admiralty	3 September 1939
Rt Hon Viscount Halifax KG GCSI GCIE TD	Secretary of State for Foreign Affairs	3 September 1939
Rt Hon Lord Hankey GCB GCMG GCVO	Minister without Portfolio	3 September 1939
Rt Hon Sir Samuel Hoare GCSI GBE CMG MP	Lord Privy Seal	3 September 1939– 3 April 1940
Rt Hon Leslie Hore-Belisha MP	Secretary of State for War	3 September 1939– 5 January 1940
Rt Hon Sir John Simon GCSI GCVO OBE KC MP	Chancellor of the Exchequer	3 September 1939
Rt Hon Oliver Stanley MC MP	Secretary of State for War	5 January 1940
Rt Hon Sir Kingsley Wood MP	Secretary of State for Air	3 September 1939– 3 April 1940

THE WAR CABINET
11 MAY 1940–
23 MAY 1945

(Where no terminal date is given the minister in question remained a member of the War Cabinet until the end of the period)

Name	Office held in War Cabinet	Dates of membership
Rt Hon Winston S Churchill MP	Prime Minister and First Lord of the Treasury, and Minister of Defence	11 May 1940
Rt Hon Sir John Anderson GCB GCSI GCIE MP	Lord President of the Council	3 October 1940–24 September 1943
	Chancellor of the Exchequer	24 September 1943
Rt Hon Clement Attlee MP	Lord Privy Seal	11 May 1940–19 February 1942
(Attlee was officially named as Deputy Prime Minister on 19 February 1942)	Secretary of State for the Dominions	19 February 1942–24 September 1943
	Lord President of the Council	24 September 1943
Rt Hon Lord Beaverbrook	Minister of Aircraft Production	2 August 1940–1 May 1941
	Minister of State	1 May 1941–29 June 1941
	Minister of Supply	29 June 1941–4 February 1942
	Minister of Production	4 February 1942–19 February 1942
Rt Hon Ernest Bevin MP	Minister of Labour and National Service	3 October 1940
Rt Hon Richard Casey DSO MC	Minister of State (resident in Middle East)	19 March 1942–23 December 1943
Rt Hon Neville Chamberlain MP	Lord President of the Council	11 May 1940–3 October 1940
Rt Hon Sir Stafford Cripps KC MP JP	Lord Privy Seal	19 February 1942–22 November 1942
Rt Hon Anthony Eden MC MP	Secretary of State for Foreign Affairs	22 December 1940
Rt Hon Arthur Greenwood MP	Minister without Portfolio	11 May 1940–22 February 1942
Rt Hon Viscount Halifax KG GCSI GCIE TD	Secretary of State for Foreign Affairs	11 May 1940–22 December 1940

63

Name	Office held in War Cabinet	Dates of membership
Captain Rt Hon Oliver Lyttelton DSO MC MP	Minister of State	29 June 1941– 19 February 1942
	Minister of State (resident in Middle East)	19 February 1942– 12 March 1942
	Minister of Production	12 March 1942
Rt Hon Herbert Morrison MP	Secretary of State for the Home Department and Minister of Home Security	22 November 1942
Rt Hon Sir Kingsley Wood MP	Chancellor of the Exchequer	3 October 1940– 19 February 1942
Rt Hon Lord Woolton CH	Minister of Reconstruction	11 November 1943

THE CHIEFS OF STAFF ▮▮▮ SEPTEMBER 1939– ▮▮▮ MAY 1945 ▮▮▮▮▮▮

(Where no terminal date is given the officer in question served until the end of the period)

First Sea Lord and Chief of the Naval Staff

Admiral of the Fleet Sir Dudley Pound GCB GCVO	June 1939–October 1943
Admiral of the Fleet Sir Andrew Cunningham Bt GCB DSO	October 1943

Chief of the Imperial General Staff

General Sir Edmund Ironside GCB CMG DSO	September 1939–June 1940
General Sir John Dill KCB CMG DSO	June 1940–December 1941
General (later Field-Marshal) Sir Alan Brooke GCB DSO	December 1941

Chief of the Air Staff

Air Chief Marshal Sir Cyril Newall GCB CMG CBE	September 1937–October 1940
Air Chief Marshal (later Marshal of the Royal Air Force) Sir Charles Portal GCB DSO MC	October 1940

Chief of Staff to the Minister of Defence

Major-General (later General) Sir Hastings Ismay KCB DSO	May 1940

Chief of Combined Operations

Vice-Admiral Lord Louis Mountbatten GCVO CB DSO	March 1942–October 1943

BIBLIOGRAPHY

Author	Title	Publisher
Burk, Kathleen (Editor)	War and the State: The Transformation of British Government, 1914–1919	Allen and Unwin, 1982
Churchill, Winston S	The Second World War, Volumes I to VI	Cassell, 1948–1954
d'Ombrain, Nicholas	War Machinery and High Policy	Oxford University Press, 1973
Ehrmann, John	Cabinet Government and War, 1890–1940	Cambridge University Press, 1958
Feiling, Keith	The Life of Neville Chamberlain	Archon, Connecticut, 1970
Gilbert, Martin	Winston S Churchill, Volumes I to V	Heinemann, 1966–1976
Gilbert, Martin	Finest Hour: Winston S Churchill, 1939–1941	Heinemann, 1983
Ismay, General the Lord	Memoirs	Heinemann, 1960
Johnson, Franklyn A	Defence by Committee: The British Committee of Imperial Defence 1885–1959	Oxford University Press, 1960
Leasor, James	War at the Top (Based on the experiences of General Sir Leslie Hollis)	Michael Joseph, 1959
Roskill, Stephen	Hankey: Man of Secrets, Volumes I to III	Collins, 1970–1974
Wheatley, Dennis	The Deception Planners: My Secret War	Hutchinson, 1980
Wheeler-Bennett, Sir John (Editor)	Action This Day: Working with Churchill	Macmillan, 1968
Wilson, S S	The Cabinet Office to 1945	HMSO, 1979

AUTHOR'S ACKNOWLEDGEMENTS ▮▮▮▮▮▮▮▮▮▮

I am deeply indebted to many people for their help in the preparation of this booklet. My special thanks are due to Mr Nigel de Lee of the Department of War Studies and International Affairs at the Royal Military Academy Sandhurst, who carried out the bulk of the initial research at the Public Record Office, and to my colleague Mr Jon Wenzel, now Curator of the Cabinet War Rooms, who subsequently uncovered a great deal of additional evidence.

The following former members of the War Cabinet Office, the Prime Minister's Private Office and the staff of the Cabinet War Rooms have given freely of their time and have contributed much useful information and advice: Mrs Joan Astley; Mr Victor Benham; Major A H Bishop; Miss D Brown; Sir John Colville; Mrs Margaret D'Arcy; Marshal of the Royal Air Force Sir William Dickson; Captain C M Drake; Air Chief Marshal Sir Alfred Earle; Sir William Gorell Barnes; Miss Betty Green; Sir Ronald Harris; Mr David Hubback; Lieutenant-General Sir Ian Jacob; Wing Commander G H Lewis; Captain J S S Litchfield; Lieutenant-Commander Ian McEwan; Mrs Olive Margerison; Sir John Martin; Mrs K M Maxwell; Miss Sheila Minto; Sir William Murrie; Mrs Margaret Paine; Sir John Peck; Mrs Margery Ransom; Group Captain Peter Riddell; Mr and Mrs Ray Smith; Mrs Joan Sneddon; Air Commodore R E de T Vintras; and Sir John Winnifrith.

I also wish to express my gratitude for the invaluable assistance I have received from Colonel C E Barrette; Mr Stephen Batchelor of Gordon Bowyer and Partners; Mrs Yolande Capper; Mr Robin Dawson of H L Dawson and Partners; Mr Ron Ferrier; Captain Godfrey French; Mr Stephen Geiss; Mr Martin Gilbert; Mr H J Gregory; Mr Charles Howard; Mr Amos E Joel Jnr of the Bell Laboratories; Mr Neil Johannesson of the British Telecom Showcase; Mr W J Milton; Mr Nicol Mutch and Mr John Ely of the Property Services Agency, Department of the Environment; Lieutenant-Colonel E C H Organ; Dr Robert Price of the Sperry Research Centre; Mr Robert Purdy; Mr Edward Rance and Mr Peter Rance; Mr Derek Robinson of the BBC; The Lady Soames; Mr H L Theobald; Mr Christiaan Truter; Mr William Turner; and Major-General D A L Wade.

Finally, I would like to acknowledge the help of all my colleagues in the Imperial War Museum who have been involved in the Cabinet War Rooms project and, in particular, that of Mrs Janet Mihell of the Department of Museum Services, who has seen this publication through the press.

Peter Simkins
Imperial War Museum   October 1983

67

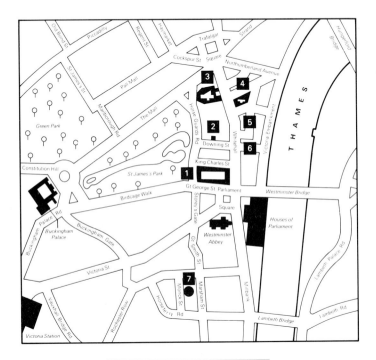

BELOW Map of the Whitehall area of London in 1939–1945 period, showing the location of the Government Offices, Great George Street (New Public Offices), in relation to other Government buildings and places mentioned in the text of this booklet.

KEY

1 Government Offices, Great George Street (New Public Offices)

2 No. 10 Downing Street

3 Admiralty

4 War Office

5 Whitehall Gardens

6 Richmond Terrace

7 'Anson'